HECATE

Witchcraft, Death
& Nocturnal Magic

HECATE

Witchcraft, Death & Nocturnal Magic

Edited and compiled
by Asenath Mason & Bill Duvendack

Temple of Ascending Flame

2021

List of Contents

Introduction

Terrifying mistress of the night and witchcraft, with serpents in her hair and a torch in her hands, surrounded by howling hounds - this is the depiction of Hecate in visual arts, ancient myths and folk legends. The cult of this ancient goddess was popular in Thrace, she had many followers among the Carians of Anatolia, and her worship was widely spread throughout Greece. It was through the Greek myths and legends that she has found her way into the culture of the West. In her ancient depictions, Hecate was portrayed as a woman sitting on a throne, three women joined at the backside (of the same age, or a maiden, nymph and crone), or one character with three heads. There were statues depicting her as a woman with three heads, of which one was human, and the other two were the head of a horse and a dog, or a lion and a bull. In some depictions she also appears with the head of a snake.

Hecate possessed many aspects and many powers. Often her cults referred to the concept of life and death, the mystical transformation through death and rebirth. She was benevolent and generous to nature and to humans, as well as ruthless and responsible for all nocturnal atrocities and destructive witchcraft. She ruled the earth, the sky and the sea, and she also decided about human fates. Her worshippers prayed to her for happiness, wealth and prosperity. In Athens, houses had a small altar in honor of Hecate and she was highly respected among the common people. According to Hesiod's *Theogony*, she was the daughter of the Titans Perses and

Asteria, and a benevolent deity who nursed the children of Zeus. Hesiod's Hecate was the favorite of the gods and humans, the goddess who always listened to and answered people's prayers. She could endow man with wealth, power and fame, protected soldiers in battles and sailors at sea. She watched over the justice in courts and granted victory in competitions. And finally, she was also associated with the moon and worshipped as the patroness of agriculture.

On the other hand, Hecate was viewed as a goddess of darkness and death. It was believed that she appeared at night at the crossroads, accompanied by dogs, ghouls and wraiths. She could assume a terrifying shape, wandered around graveyards and heralded misfortune to all who saw her. Therefore, one of her names was Antaia ("she who meets"). She was also called Trivia as she appeared at three roads crossing one another. In many cultures, crossroads are thought to represent the earthly point where worlds and dimensions meet and intersect: the realm of spirits and the world of matter, the place of gods and the mundane reality of humans, the earthly and the divine. During her nocturnal wanderings, Hecate was extremely dangerous and people stayed away from places where she could appear, because it was believed that she brought death to those that she encountered. But those who dared to seek her, she always pointed in the right way - the one that should be chosen from the three crossing roads, the path of initiation into her dark mysteries.

Hecate was often seen in desolate places: on tops of mountains, in the depth of forests, and in forgotten groves. Her kingdom was that of wild animals: hounds, wolves, dears, and serpents. Her witchcraft often included mysteries of transformation into a beast, a practice resembling the shamanic tradition of shape-shifting. Like the goddess, who assumed shapes of animals herself, a follower of her path could shape-shift into bestial creatures associated with her lore. In her retinue one could find Empusa, the fearful ghoul feeding on human flesh and haunting her prey under the disguise of a beautiful woman.

Hecate was also a goddess of the underworld and a psychopomp - she led the souls of the deceased to the gates of Hades, guarded by the hellish dog Cerberus. This connection between her and the hound of the underworld is further examined in one of the essays included in this book. She was also believed to rule over vengeance and atonement. At the crossroads, her worshippers left cakes and honey as offerings, and sometimes also animals were sacrificed, especially black dogs. Her cult was unlike the worship of other deities celebrated by open, public festivals. Offerings to Hecate were left secretly at night for her and her servants and companions: wild animals and the creatures of the night. Moreover, it was believed that the celebrants should not turn back or look when she came to claim them because this sight was so terrifying that it could scare them to death.

However, Hecate was, above all, the patroness of witches and the goddess of dark magic. She endowed them with the power over the forces of nature, revealed the secrets of herbs, and taught how to prepare magical potions. In the myth of the Golden Fleece, Medea, a witch and priestess of Hecate, gathers narcotic herbs, with which she puts to sleep the sleepless dragon guarding the fleece so that Jason can kill the beast and complete his quest. Hecate was also the mistress of necromancy and funeral magic. To her followers she appeared with torches in her hands, or in an animal shape - a mare, hound, or wolf. She led her adepts through the path of darkest and deepest layers of the irrational. Her cult was persecuted by patriarchal religions because it involved practices that seemed devious and dangerous, especially those connected with the powers of female sexuality. Women who worshipped Hecate used witchcraft to increase their sexual attractiveness and to get whatever they wanted. We can see that in the myth of Medea, too. To get what she wants, she does not hesitate to perform acts that may seem atrocious, even at her times, like killing her brother only to distract her father from pursuing her and Jason after stealing the Golden Fleece. She murders the boy, cuts his body into pieces and scatters them on the road, so that her father might thus be delayed by gathering the limbs of his child. Her story is full of manipulation, violence and witchcraft used to accomplish her goals and take revenge on those who have wronged her. The cult of Hecate was therefore associated with the cult of female power, and thus, a threat to patriarchal structures of the community. In this sense, Hecate was one of the "darkest" goddesses of the Western pantheon. Her cult is the *via sinistra*, the exploration of the dark side of human nature, the wild element, the dark instinct of the primordial Left-Hand-Path traditions.

In ancient Greece, Hecate was also associated with the moon and thus considered a goddess of moonlight. That is why, she was called Mene, the name deriving from Selene, the goddess of the moon and the underworld. Her mysteries can therefore be associated with the female cycle, which has been linked with the moon phases since earliest antiquity. Hecate, however, was a chthonic goddess. One of her main attributes is a key that opens the gate of Hades, while her torch lights up the dark corridors and tunnels of the underworld. She is the guide who leads adepts through the kingdom of the dead, the psychopomp of the souls and those who travel beyond the veil of life and death, the goddess of illumination, sometimes even depicted as a living flame, illuminating the darkness of obscurity and oblivion.

In literature, witches often summon her name in their spells and rites. In Shakespeare's *Macbeth*, Hecate is the Queen of Witches invoked by the "weird sisters" in their grim prophesies. Shakespeare often mentions this mysterious goddess in his magic-themed plays such as *Macbeth* or *Midsummer Night's Dream*. In the contemporary drama she is commonly linked with witchcraft and the night. Also *The Witch* from the title of the play by the English playwright Thomas Middleton is called Hecate. This dark goddess is often described as a personification of black magic. This image is rooted in the medieval tradition, when Hecate was the goddess of death and moonlight, the mistress of the dead, the Wild Hunt, warriors, and presided over nocturnal gathering of witches and their malevolent spells.

The name "Hecate" itself is of unknown origin. It has been suggested that it might mean "the far-reaching one." There is also a resemblance between the word "Hecate" and the Egyptian term "hekau," meaning "magic," which is explored in another essay included here, or it can also be a derivative from the name of the Egyptian Heqet, the frog-headed goddess of childbirth. According to Robert Graves, her name means "hundred" and refers to the Great Year of hundred lunar months, when once ruled the Sacred King. In his *Greek Myths* he observes that his blood was the symbol of the earth's rebirth. Hecate has many other titles as well. Apart from the above-mentioned, she was also called Aphrattos ("Unnamed"), Pandeina ("Terrifying"), Phosophoros ("Bearing Light," a title often associated with Lucifer), Apotropaia ("She who turns away"), or Soteira ("Savior").

Among other goddesses, she was identified with Artemis, Selene, Demeter, or Persephone. It was she who told Demeter about Persephone's abduction by Hades into the underworld. Through her marriage to Hades, Persephone became the mistress of the cyclic changes in nature - in late autumn she descends to the underworld, which marks the beginning of winter and the seasonal death of nature. In the spring she returns, bringing new life into the world. When she emerges from the land of the dead, Hecate comes forth to greet her, and thus becomes her companion in the symbolic process of nature's death and rebirth. As the goddess of magic and dark rites, she can also be linked with the Celtic Cerridwen, the mistress of witchcraft, whose main attribute is the cauldron of wisdom. The iconographic image of a witch as a woman brewing a magical potion in a cauldron is the re-enactment of this ancient myth. The witch's potion was the source of great knowledge, unknown to non-initiates. In *Celtic Myth and Magick*, Edain McCoy describes a legend in which when Cerridwen's servant tasted a few drops of her elixir, he gained access to profound knowledge, discovered poetic talents in himself, and developed the ability to see the past and the future events.

Initiation into the mysteries of Hecate is the descent into the personal underworld, where the knowledge of our origin, ancestral heritage and forgotten talents lies hidden, awaiting to be re-discovered. Hecate leads us through dark paths to the gates of hell, where the terrifying Cerberus guards the long forgotten secrets of power and immortality. The key to the door is in the hand of the goddess and her torch is the flame of illumination, shining into the depth of the Initiate's soul. In the Draconian Tradition, she is the guardian of the mystical point of crossing, where all worlds, planes, and dimensions meet and become one. She is the first initiatrix, the psychopomp, and the sentinel who meets the aspiring Initiate at the Crossroads of the Worlds, leading us into the Womb of the Dragon through the gateways of the Nightside.

This anthology contains all those portrayals of Hecate and many more, introducing the reader to the magic and mythology of this mysterious goddess. Here you will find descriptions of personal gnosis revealed through the work of authors featured in this book, as well as references to her appearance in ancient lore and magic of old times. Like the other anthologies by the Temple of Ascending Flame, all this is written from the perspective of the Draconian Initiate, involving a modern approach suitable for the practitioner of the Left Hand Path.

Let us then begin the journey into the underworld, where the knowledge of ourselves and our universe lies concealed, waiting to be claimed, absorbed and transformed into our personal power.

Sigil of Hecate as the Lady of the Crossroads and the Guide to the Underworld

Hecate: The Goddess of Magic, Mysteries & Witchcraft

"I am the Great Mother Binah, worshipped by men since creation and existing before their consciousness. I am the primal female force: boundless and eternal.

I am the Goddess of the Moon, chaste Diana, the Lady of all magic. The winds and moving leaves sing my name.

I wear the crescent moon upon my brow, and my feet rest among the starry heavens. I am mysteries yet unsolved; a path newly set upon; I am a field yet untouched by the plow.

Rejoice in me and be free.

I am the blessed mother Demeter, the gracious lady of the harvest. I am clothed with the deep, cool wonder of the Earth and the gold of the fields, heavy with grain.

By me, the tides of the Earth are ruled; all things come to fruit according to my season. I am refuge and healing.

I am the mother, giving life to the Universe.

I have been with you from the beginning, and I am with you for eternity.

Worship me as Hecate, the unbroken cycle of death and rebirth. I am the wheel, the shadow of the Moon. I rule the tides of men and give release and renewal to weary souls.

Though the darkness of death is my domain, the joy of birth is my gift. I know all things and have attained all wisdom.

I am the Goddess of the Moon, the Earth, the Seas. My names and strengths are many. All magic and power is mine; all peace and wisdom comes through me.

I call thy soul; arise and come. I am that which is attained at the end of all desire.

I am Diana."

(Song of the Goddess, Book of Shadows*)*

Hecate (pronounced as "he-ka-tee") is believed by many scholars to have originated in Caria, western Anatolia, as proved by the fact that proper names compounded with her name are commonplace in this district and rare elsewhere. Her role as a goddess in Caria is, however, not clearly known. She is often depicted in the company of snakes, either girdled or flanked by them and sometimes she is shown with her three-headed dog Cerberus. Apuleius, in the eleventh book of *The Golden Ass,* attributes the following statement to the goddess: "Behold I, moved by thy prayers, am present with thee; I, who am Nature, the parent of things, the queen of all the elements, the primordial progeny of ages, the supreme of Divinities, the sovereign of the spirits of the dead, the first of the celestials, and the uniform resemblance of Gods and Goddesses. I, who rule by my nod the luminous summits of the heavens, the salubrious breezes of the sea, and the deplorable silences of the realms beneath, and whose one divinity the whole orb of the earth venerates under a manifold form, by different rites and a variety of appellations. Hence the primogenial Phrygians call me Pessinuntica, the mother of the Gods, the Attic Aborigines, Cecropian Minerva; the floating Cyprians, Paphian Venus; the arrow-bearing Cretans, Diana Dictynna; the three-tongued Sicilians, Stygian Proserpine; and the Eleusinians, the ancient Goddess Ceres. Some also call me Juno, others Bellona, others Rhamnusia, and many Hecate."

Hecate is historically associated with the infernal fires of the underworld. She carried blazing torches with which she guided souls through the underworld, and her followers regularly made offerings to her in fiery pits in the earth. Her representation of holding a torch is a trivial way to represent fire, but most importantly, this fact stands for the transcendence of all limitations, the holder of the light. One meaning of Hecate's name is "influence from afar" or "the distant one," which refers to her ability to affect change over a vast expanse, as well as having a uniquely impartial vantage point. For her, nothing is hidden, and there are no boundaries. She walks freely through the mazes of our lives and can help pinpoint where inner fears have taken hold, and thus Hecate can help you look within and bring awareness and light whenever you are at your darkest moments.

Hecate is a powerful goddess with chthonic associations who is the patron of magic and witchcraft. She has three aspects: goddess of fertility and plenty, goddess of the moon, and queen of the night, ghosts, and shades. She possesses infernal power, roaming the earth at night in wild pursuit, with a pack of dogs, and an entourage of dead souls. She is the cause of nightmares and insanity and is so terrifying that many ancients referred to her only as "The Nameless One." She is the goddess of the dark of the moon, the destroyer of life, but also the restorer of life. In one myth, she turns into a bear and kills her own son, then revives him to life. In her dark aspect, she wears a necklace made of a phallus and testicles with her hair made of twisting snakes, which, as do the snakes of Medusa, petrify those who gaze upon them.

Hecate is the goddess of all crossroads, gazing in three directions at the same time. In ancient times, sorcerers gathered at crossroads to pay homage to her. Three-headed statues of her were set up at many road intersections, and secret rites were performed under the full moon to appease her. Statues of Hecate carrying torches or swords were also erected in front of homes to keep evil spirits at bay.

Hecate was introduced to Greece as early as the early archaic age (7-8th century BCE). Propaganda was resorted to on behalf of her cult, as is apparent in the *Homeric Hymn to Demeter*, in which she is praised as omnipotent. In Greece, she was always the goddess of witchcraft and sorcery who walked at the crossroads on moonless nights, accompanied by evil ghosts and barking dogs. Offerings were thrown out to her at the crossroads, and her image was triple because she had to look in three directions. She was often called Enodia (she of the roads), and at all events, Hecate was accepted by the Greeks because there was a place for a goddess of witchcraft and ghosts. Her popularity is accounted for by this fact, and it proves that base superstitions were only too common among the Greeks. It may be added that Hecate, the goddess of witchcraft, was one of the deities to whom women were especially devoted. The reason for her popularity with women is that in ancient Greece sorcery and witchcraft were the concern of women. The image of the triple Hecate was frequently erected in front of the house and at the crossroads. Aristophanes tells us that when a woman left her house, she always made a prayer to Hecate because a power that can produce ghosts and magical evils can also avert them.

Hecate is also seen in the Chaldean Oracles, which emphasized the goddess in a more prevailing role than she had ever been seen before, that of a savior (Soteira), and a cosmic soul. She was described as being both the "substance and origin" of symbols and dreams and also the supreme goddess incorporating the Titan Rhea, who had been the Greek Mother of the Gods. In these oracles, she became the source of souls and virtues, bestowing her power on the seeker who approached her appropriately. The seeker concentrated on union with the gods to achieve perfection and emphasized spiritual development rather than mundane concerns. The Chaldean Oracles also described Hecate's fires as winding or enwrapping. The Gnostics embraced the concept of a fire snake as the embodiment of Sophia (or wisdom), which rose up the spine and enabled the practitioner to cross the threshold and ascend to spirit.

"Astarte, Aphrodite, Ashtoreth
Giver of life and bringer of death;
Hera in Heaven, on earth, Persephone;
Levanah of the tides, and Hecate
All these am I, and they are seen in me.
Mine is the kingdom of Persephone,
The inner earth where lead the pathways three.
Who drinks the waters of that hidden well!
Shall see the things whereof he dare not tell
Shall tread the shadowy path that leads to me
Diana of the Ways and Hecate,
Selene of the Moon, Persephone."
(*The Sea Priestess,* Dion Fortune)

MODERN RELIGIONS AND OTHER BELIEFS

Hecate is known as the goddess with ten thousand designations and is transmuted by Christianity into the Virgin Mary, for although she gave birth to many (chief among them the Sun), she still remained a virgin. Christianity demonizes the entity Hecate, calling her one of the five demonic archons (rulers) who torment souls. We, however, observe many useful materials borrowed from Hecate's worship to include in personal practices. For example, we see the term Lampades, originally used for Hecate's torch-bearing nymphs, being used to refer to the seven archangels who stand in the presence of God, likewise the title of Kleidouchos (key-bearer), which may represent Hecate as the guardian of the entrance to the paradisiacal Elysian Fields in the underworld being appropriated for Saint Peter as holding the keys to heaven.

In the Luciferian current, she is sometimes seen as the mother of Lucifer. In this interpretation, the goddess creates Lucifer when she parts herself to become two separate beings, one of light, the other, herself, remaining dark. She also carries with her the association of Saturn as his lady, Fate. In this association, Saturn, of course, rules time, and therefore both life and death, or creation and destruction, and all of the processes of change that take place between. Operating as Fate, Hecate, therefore, decrees the orderly passage of these processes via cause and effect. Thus, she is both the Great Mother and the Cruel Mother of our lore.

In rites of Draconian magic, she is the guide through mysteries of the underworld and the first initiator on the path, leading us into the Womb of Lilith through the gateways of the Nightside. My working with Hecate started when I was going through initiatory stages into Draconian magic by the Temple of Ascending Flame. I found the goddess to be motherly but cruel at the same time. She told me that through fire and force I had to be purified and polished, a process that was to shave off my ego and mishaps, forcing me toward evolution, and then basking me in her divine light. Altogether, when Hecate comes into your life, subtle changes start happening from within and without, and the changes can be easy or difficult as the rotten and the negative parts are cut off from your life. These changes can then become dramatic, traumatic, and sometimes painful, but they are all necessary for your spiritual growth.

AFRICAN SPIRITUALITY AND VODOU TRADITIONS

Those in Ethiopia who claimed to be illuminated by the incipient rays of the divine Sun and the Egyptians worshipped Hecate under her true name, "Queen Isis." Occasionally Isis is represented as a bird. She often carries in one hand the *crux ansata*, the symbol of eternal life, and in the other, the flowered scepter, symbolic of her authority.

"I, Isis, am all that has been, that is or shall be; no mortal Man hath ever had me unveiled."

Isis, as she is known in Africa as Queen Auset, became one of the most celebrated of all goddesses. She controls the planets in the air, winds of the sea, and the silence of hell. Her divinity is adored in all the world in various manners and different customs and by many people. Originating in Upper Egypt, this black goddess became the face of women throughout the lands. In his book, *Metamorphoses*, Apuleius designates Auset as a conglomerate of all goddesses of the world and that no goddess exists without being her. She is the Queen of the Sky, Queen of Queens, Lady of all Ladies, natural mother of all things, mistress of all elements, governor of all progeny, chief of all divine things, principal of gods, and light of all goddesses. He then describes the deity as a powerful figure coming out of the sea with an abundance of hair and many garlands of flowers stuck in her hair. She has a disk in the shape of a small mirror on her head, and in one hand, she holds the light of the moon and serpents, and in the other, blades of corn. Her silk robe shimmers with many colors. She bears with her flowers and fruits, a tumbrel of brass, and a cup of gold. Furthermore, her mouth holds the serpent Aspis, and her sweet feet are covered with shoes laced with palms.

Further, down in Southwest Egypt, a close relation to Queen Isis (Auset) of Egypt is seen with water deities found primarily in the Vodou tradition practiced in Benin and Togo. These deities are collectively known as *Mami Wata,* whose manifestations and variations are found in at least 20 African countries, the Caribbean, and North America. The name Mami Wata is thought to mean "mother of the waters," which can be traced back to ancient Egypt: *ma* or *mama*, meaning "truth" or "wisdom," and *uati* for "water." Just like Queen Isis, Mami Wata has designated splendid names; for example, among the Igbo, she is *Ezenwaanyi* ("Queen of Women"), *Nnekwunwenyi* ("Honorable Woman"), *Ezebelamiri* ("Queen who lives in the Waters"), *Nwaanyi mara mma* ("More than Beautiful Woman"). Among other names, she is known as *Mamba Muntu*

(Crocodile Person) in Congo; Watramama in Suriname and Guyana; Mamadjo in Grenada; Yemanya in Brazil and Cuba; La Sirène, Erzulie, and Simbi in Haiti; and Lamanté in Martinique. Mami Wata deities are the source of earthly wisdom, human creativity, genius, divine inspiration, and sacred paths to enlightenment. Mami Wata shrines in Benin are seen to incorporate icons from Hindu, Muslim, and European traditions, images of the Catholic Black Madonna and child, the Hindu Lakshmi, goddess of wealth, beauty, and happiness, and Islam's al-Buraq, the winged horse with a woman's head that the prophet Mohammed rode from Mecca to Jerusalem. Also similar to Apuleius' description of Queen Isis (Auset), the deity Mami Wata appears as a beautiful creature, half woman, half fish, with long hair and a light brown complexion, and she lives in a gorgeous underwater world. She is often depicted with a snake around her waist or across her shoulders or with a comb and a mirror. The snake is the immortal messenger of deities and a symbol of divination, whereas the comb and mirror are symbols of her beauty or vanity. Mami Wata's colors are red and white to reflect her dual nature as aggressive but healing and nurturing.

Still in western Africa, the Fon in Benin and Yoruba people in Nigeria share a god that waits at the crossroads and acts as a divine messenger, an intercessor between gods and man, and a teacher of healing and baneful magic, a trickster given to pranks that can be entertaining, educational, lethal, or any combination thereof. We see a stunning resemblance between Hecate and this god of the crossroads, but in this case, Hecate appears as a masculine force. The Yoruba call him Esu, or Elegbara, the messenger of divine authority, and the Fon know him as Legba. The crossroads is a pervasive idea that suggests a point where good and evil, humanity and divinity, the living and the dead, the night and the day, and all other contradictions, opposites, and situations involving decisions must meet. At this point, there exists an intermediary to open the way, to provide humans with a choice, and to teach wisdom at the gate. Legba is that intermediary and is generally featured as a large, erect, and prominently displayed penis that stands guard at many doorways and village gates. During ceremonies in his honor, dancers wear palm frond skirts in which are hidden wooden phalluses, ten to eighteen inches long. In some images, Hecate is depicted with many hands, and one of them is holding a phallus. This, in turn, relates Hecate and Legba of the Fons as one spiritual force appearing diverse in different areas.

"The person who navigates the crossroads successfully, in African belief, will be rewarded with the wisdom that is reserved for the one who respects the crossroads."
(Molefi Kete Asante)

In Caribbean Vodou traditions, this same masculine force, as a deity of the crossroads, is worshipped as Elegua in Cuba and Exu in Brazil. In Brazil, however, there also appears a feminine force with a parallel relation to Hecate, "the Lady of the Night," *Pomba Gira*. Pomba Gira, as an Afro Brazillian spirit of the crossroads, graveyard, and witchcraft, is a consort of Exu and a messenger of Orixia (sprits of creation). This could be the same force of Hecate that personifies both male and female sexualities. Exu and Elegua appear as a lively trickster and a mischievous young boy. In Haiti, however, this spirit of the crossroads appears as a shabby older man dressed in rags, and he is called Papa Legba. Papa Legba usually manifests in the Rada service of Haitian Vodou as an old man leaning on a crutch and accompanied by one or more dogs. But although Legba may appear to be a feeble old man, Vodouisants believe that none of the spirits can "come down" to this world without his assistance. He is the gatekeeper and the catalyst; he stands in every time and every place where two ways are joined. Hecate in many myths is associated with dogs. She is sometimes seen holding keys to the gates of the underworld. These attributes further enhance her similarity with Papa Legba as they do with the West African god of the crossroads. As it is noticed with the followers of Legba in Benin and Haiti, Greek worshipers of Hecate also kept their shrines near the doorway or gate.

BIBLIOGRAPHY

Martin P. Nilsson. *Greek Popular Religion,* 1940. Pages 80-97.

Burkert, Walter. *Greek Religion.* Cambridge, Cambridge University Press, 1985.

Johnston, Sarah Iles. *Hecate Soteira.* Georgia, Scholars Press, 1990.

Molefi Kete Asante. *Encyclopedia of African religions,* 2009.

The Golden Ass by Lucius Apuleius "Africanus" translated by William Adlington in 1566.

Frank, B. "Permitted and Prohibited Wealth: Commodity-Possessing Spirits, Economic Morals, and the Goddess Mami Wata in West Africa." *Ethnology* 34 (1995), 331–346.

Hecate: Goddess of the Crossroads

Three Faces of Hecate

This series of workings was conducted as an open project by the Temple of Ascending Flame in the spring of 2014. It is centered on Hecate, her ancient myths and symbols, and her role in Draconian self-initiatory magic. In this text, I have included both the original workings and the description of results reported by the participants. It can be done in its original form, on six days in a row, or you can adjust it as you wish, and e.g. explore each of the masks on one day only. I do not recommend condensing it to one day, though. Every working provides a different glimpse into the multitude of Hecate's aspects, and each of them needs time to manifest in the life of the practitioner. Therefore, feel free to explore the three faces of the goddess for as long as you wish, but leave enough time for introspection and manifestation of their results in your day-to-day life.

Each daily working contains different elements. The first meditation will open you for the energies of the goddess and invite her into your personal temple. The following meditations will successively guide you into her mysteries, taking you on the journey into your personal underworld. The invocation of the goddess will integrate the whole experience in intimate communion with her timeless essence, and the last day's ritual is left to your personal choice. The purpose of this series of workings is to introduce you to the mysteries of Hecate as the Lady of Transformation and the Goddess of the

Crossroads through her Draconian/Ophidian current and the mystical journey into the underworld within.

"Faces" of Hecate

Initiation into the mysteries of Hecate is the descent into the underworld that we all have inside us. The goddess leads us through dark paths to the gate of "hell," where the terrifying Cerberus guards the long forgotten secrets of power and immortality. The key to the door is in the hand of the goddess, and her torch is the flame of illumination, shining into the depth of the adept's soul. In rites of Draconian magic, she is the guide into the mysteries of witchcraft and the first initiatrix on the path of the Nightside. Her symbol is the key and the torch, or two torches, associated with nocturnal journeys, entrance-ways and illumination, and the dagger, which is the tool of separation, representing the mystery of liberating the soul from the mundane body.

In ancient depictions, Hecate was often presented as a triple goddess, with three bodies or three heads. Sometimes these heads were human, representing her manifold and mystical nature. Other times they were animal heads symbolic of her divine powers and the initiatory character of her rites. Various pictures and statues present her with the head of a dog, serpent, boar, or cow. This project is centered on her bestial totems typified by the serpent, dog and horse.

The serpent is the symbol of metamorphosis, transformation, and shape-shifting. It represents the Ophidian current of the goddess and her power of altering consciousness in order to make the journey into the Nightside possible. We cannot enter the underworld in the mundane form - we have to leave it behind. This shift in consciousness occurs at Hecate's Crossroads and is necessary to travel into the realms of the Nightside. The gate opened at the Crossroads is the gate within, leading into the inner darkness, the personal underworld, where we have to let these forces in, embrace them and become one with them. This is the mystery of Hecate's initiatory rites. The serpent is also symbolic of poison. Transformation occurs through poisoning consciousness and initiating the change within. That is why Hecate is often associated with poisonous herbs used in rites of magic to alter consciousness, such as aconite or belladonna, which separate the soul from the body and allow for the journey to worlds and dimensions that cannot be accessed in the flesh. The serpent is the first "face," or aspect, of Hecate explored in this project. This work includes a meditation on entering the Crossroads of the Worlds and opening the gate to the Nightside.

The dog is the oldest symbol and companion of Hecate. In ancient sources and depictions, she is commonly attended by dogs, especially female, and her appearance was believed to be heralded by the barking or howling of dogs. Also, dogs were regular sacrificial animals in her cults. The goddess herself was sometimes called the "she-dog" or "bitch," and she had two ghostly dogs as servants by her side. These dogs are symbolic of her chthonic powers, and she is also the mistress of Cerberus, the three-headed beast-dog who guards the entrance to the underworld. Like Cerberus, dogs in ancient myths are guardians and guides standing by the gateways to the realm of the dead. Such is also the role of this "face" of Hecate. She is both the guardian of the gate to the underworld and the guide (*psychopompos*) of souls travelling there. She opens the gateways at the crossroads and guides the traveler into the labyrinths of the Nightside. In meditation exploring this aspect of the goddess, you will set on a visual journey into your personal underworld in order to face your inner darkness and look into the mirror of your soul.

The horse in ancient mythologies is a symbol of movement, transition, and otherworldly journeys. It is the vehicle used by the adept to travel through worlds above and worlds below through the axis of the universe. It is the driving force and the symbol of the journey. The horse is also associated with funerary symbolism, and in funerary rites, hearses are drawn by horses, thus assisting the deceased in their journey to the grave, the chthonic womb of the earth. This has a double meaning, as the womb of the earth is the place of both death and resurrection - all life returns to earth and turns to dust, and all vegetation springs from the earth. The horse, or mare, is one of the main symbolic animals of Hecate. This aspect of the goddess represents the initiatory journey in which the soul, free from bonds of the flesh, travels to the underworld and returns transformed, possessing knowledge and wisdom that can only be found in these dark regions. In this working, you will travel into the depths of your soul, crossing the border between the mundane and otherworldly, conscious and unconscious, waking and sleeping. It also includes assuming an Ophidian/Draconian form in which you will pass through the gate. This meditation will be followed by a dream-working.

Hecate has many names and epithets. The ones chosen for this project are *Trimorphis* (three-formed), *Trioditis* (of the crossroads), *Enodia* (on the way), *Chthonia* (of the underworld), and *Propylaia* (before the gate). These names, derived from ancient sources, will be used in mantras and invocations throughout the project.

PREPARATION

Prepare your ritual space in the way you feel is suitable for this work. You may put statues, images, or sigils that represent Hecate on your altar - these can be ancient depictions, modern images, or simply your personal seals or drawings. You may decorate the altar by placing offerings - roses (dried flowers work best for the chthonic/underworld goddesses), wine symbolizing the blood of the Lunar Goddess, green candles, or other offerings associated with Hecate. You may also choose to focus on the sigil alone, without any other decorations - this choice is entirely up to you. For meditations, you will need the sigil provided on page 13, big enough to gaze into comfortably. It should be painted in colors associated with the

Draconian/Ophidian current: red, golden, and black - a golden seal on black background, or black sigil on gold - all these will work fine for these workings. Another option is to use emerald green colors - for the background or the sigil itself. You will also need black candles, although you can have a few green or golden candles, too.

In ancient sources, Hecate is the "blood-eating goddess," and blood is the traditional offering given to the chthonic, underworld deities. Therefore, we will also use blood in this project. The sigil used in this work *should* be anointed and activated with your own blood. It is not absolutely necessary, though, and if the idea of offering a few drops of your blood puts you off, you do not have to do it in this particular project. Initiatory work on the Draconian Path, however, especially in the ritual system of the Temple of Ascending Flame, often requires the blood of the Initiate. If you find such practices unacceptable, perhaps this path is not for you. Think about it before starting these workings. Another important thing is that the only blood used here should be your own. Even though ancient practices of witchcraft and traditional cults of Hecate included animal sacrifice, such practices are not encouraged here or in the work of the Temple in general. You must remember that Hecate is also the goddess of birth, associated with growth and nurture, and protector of animals, and a sacrifice of life is not always welcome in her rites. I personally believe that the best blood to sacrifice is always your own. In this project, you can make the blood offering on each day, or you can do it only on the first day to activate the sigil - this is up to you. It is enough to offer just a few drops; no larger amounts are needed. For this, you will need a ritual blade - a dagger, knife, or sword - a simple razor or lancet will do as well.

DAY 1
Meditation with Hecate's Sigil and Mantra

If possible, perform this working outdoors, at the crossroads, in the forest, or a in quiet, desolate place. If not, try at least to take a walk to such a place before the working and remain there for a while, calling for the goddess and possibly leaving an offering of your choice.

Then sit in a comfortable position and put the sigil in front of you. Light the candles and burn aromatic incense, such as sandalwood or frankincense. Anoint the sigil with your blood and focus all your attention on it. See how the lines become charged and activated with your life substance. Visualize the sigil glowing and flashing with emerald-green light, and at the same time chant the mantra:

HEKATE TRIMORPHIS TRIODITIS ENODIA

Keep gazing at the sigil until you can easily memorize and visualize its shape. Then, close your eyes and recall the image in your inner mind. Focus your inner sight on the shape of the sigil and see it forming in front of you, on the black canvas of the Void. At this point, you can keep chanting the mantra or continue the practice in silence. When the vision of the sigil becomes solid, imagine it changing, shifting into other shapes, unlocking the gateways of your mind, opening the doors to the Nightside, and showing you objects, entities, landscapes, and scenes. Let the visions flow freely and open yourself for the experience. Send the message through the sigil and ask Hecate for her presence and guidance on the journey to the underworld. Invite her to your ritual space and into the temple of flesh. When you feel it is time to end the meditation, return to your mundane consciousness, blow out the candles, and finish the working.

The Ophidian current of the goddess may already manifest in a strong way through this basic meditation with the sigil.

As the symbol is changing and morphing, many practitioners see the circle, tridents, and the pentagram assuming other shapes or being arranged in many different ways, opening access to the energies of the goddess. The circle is often seen as changing into a snake - the Ouroboros serpent devouring its tail. The tridents may change into snakes as well, and the whole sigil becomes a swirling vortex. The crescent moons assume the form of the moon in all phases, reflecting the lunar nature of Hecate's energies. It is also not uncommon to see the sigil emanating flames or sparkles of fiery energy. In visions and meditations, it takes the form of the astral gateway - the pentagram becomes a portal, and the moons and tridents point the directions of the journey. There are three roads, three gates, and three moons, reflecting the threefold nature of the goddess. The crossing point seems located in none of the worlds but in between them - where space and time does not exist, where cardinal points and directions make no sense and all merge into one. This feeling of being suspended in time and space may be experienced as disorienting and nauseating, causing dizziness and sensations in the heart chakra - the meeting point of the energies. If you experience this kind of imbalance, ground yourself (you will find many grounding exercises in my *Draconian Ritual Book*) and do not proceed to the next working until you find yourself back in balance.

DAY 2
Opening of the Crossroads

Start this working in the same way as the day before: prepare the temple, light the candles and burn incense. Pour red wine into the chalice and put it on the altar. Then sit in a comfortable position and put the sigil in front of you, focusing all your attention on the image. Again, visualize the sigil glowing and flashing with Hecate's emerald-green energy. At the same time, chant the words of calling:

Hecate Trioditis, meet me at the crossroads, and reveal to me
the secrets of the Night.
With your key, I open the gates to the underworld!

As you keep chanting, feel how the atmosphere in your ritual space thickens, and the energies flowing through the sigil fill your temple and sharpen your senses. Drink the sacrament from the chalice and let it fill you with the immortal essence of the goddess. Then close your eyes and begin the visual journey to the crossroads.

Visualize yourself in a dark forest at night. The forest is old, there are many withered trees, stumps covered with moss, bones of animals scattered on the ground. At the same time, it seems alive, and you feel that you are not alone - you can see the eyes of wild animals or forest spirits flashing in the dark. The wind blowing through tree branches resembles whispering voices, and you can also hear the hissing of serpents beckoning you to go deep into the woods and dogs barking and howling from afar. There is a path in front of you, and you follow the voices that guide you to the Crossroads of the Worlds.

At the end of the path, you reach the three crossing pathways, and you notice the goddess standing there, dressed in a black hooded robe. You cannot see her face, but you can feel her piercing gaze reaching into the depths of your soul. She stands by the fire, which is pale-white, shining with ghastly light and casting living shadows that move and dance around her. As you approach, she gives you a chalice filled with magical potion. The chalice is simple and carved in bone. The potion is pitch-black and thick. When you drink it, you can feel fire arising at the base of your spine and spreading over the whole body in waves of pain and pleasure.

The goddess lowers her hood, and now you can see her face and look into her eyes. She has a serpent head with glowing reptilian eyes. Open yourself to whatever may come now. Communicate with the goddess. Let her guide you through the vision, and when it is over, return to your mundane consciousness and close the working.

The serpent aspect of Hecate explored in this working usually comes many visions of her Ophidian current. She is seen in the form of the serpent, with serpent head only, or surrounded by snakes - usually black or green. After drinking the potion from the chalice, you may experience the feeling of being transformed into a serpent yourself, dancing and swaying around her fire. Sometimes other forest spirits join the dance. These spirits are usually described as female or appear in the shape of women and include ghosts, wraiths, phantoms, and other apparitions. You may also see the goddess transforming into a huge serpent and devouring you - in this case, the entrance to the underworld is through her body itself. Snakes also act as guides to the crossroads, and you may see them leading you to the meeting place in the forest.

The goddess herself appears with a lot of Ophidian and Draconian imagery. Sometimes she is surrounded by moons and waters. Apart from her serpent-form, she may appear in this working as a black shadow, a woman in a long black dress, or she is naked and black. Her appearance is connected not only to the Ophidian current but also to death energies and the death principle symbolized by her role of the guide to the underworld. Visions received in this working also embrace the image of the sigil, and you may see the pentagram as a part of the landscape, marking the portal to the underworld. There are also visions of the portal as made of snakes or being a black spiraling vortex. The torches seen in the sigil are seen in meditations as well, marking the crossing ways and pointing the path to the goddess. Other visions include skulls, ruins, old abandoned buildings, dark forests, green waters, kteis-shaped portals, and caves - all this related to the lunar feminine imagery connected with the symbolism of the goddess. The kteis-shaped entrance is a reference to the Eye of the Dragon and the Draconian current. Some practitioners describe the entrance to the underworld as the jaws of a snake or a dragon, with sharp rocks looking like teeth of a beast. Finally, there are also visions of the passage to the underworld as a long hallway filled with misty astral waters, which brings associations with the river Lethe from the Greek myths - the further you walk, the more detached from the world you feel. The door to the underworld is also sometimes seen with a triangle and a golden eye imprinted on its black surface, which is another reference to the Eye of the Dragon, or the Eye of Lucifer, the center of awakened consciousness.

DAY 3
Descent into the Underworld

Like the day before, start the meditation with preparing the temple, candles, incense, and the sacrament. Again, sit in a comfortable position and put the sigil in front of you, focusing all your attention on the image. Visualize it glowing and flashing with sparkles of the emerald-green energy of the goddess. At the same time, chant the words of calling:

Hecate Propylaia, let me enter your darkly splendid world.
With your torch, I illuminate my way through the night!

Keep chanting until you sense the change in the atmosphere in your ritual space and feel ready to continue the working. Drink the sacrament from the chalice and let it fill you with the immortal essence of the goddess. Then close your eyes and continue your visual journey from the previous day.

Start the meditation where you finished the day before - return to the crossroads and drink the potion given to you by the goddess. Now envision the goddess with a dog's head and burning eyes. As you feel the fire arising within and you gaze into her eyes, feel her divine essence entering you and merging with your consciousness. For a while, everything becomes black, and the whole scene disappears. Then you are back in the forest, standing at the crossroads and facing an entrance to a dark cave hidden among the trees. The cave is a portal leading down into the underworld. As you enter the cave, you notice black stairs carved in stone, leading into the bowels of the earth. In your left hand, you are holding a torch. You can use it to light up the darkness while you are descending the stairs. Envision shadows moving on the walls of the corridor and hear their whispering voices, inviting you to go down, deeper and deeper.

When you reach the end of the stairs, you find yourself in a fire-lit hallway, standing at a huge, ornamented gate. It is guarded by Cerberus, the monstrous three-headed dog who has a snake for a tail and countless snake heads on his back. You reach to your pocket – you find there a key and a lash. You strike the earth with the lash, and the hound starts to obey you. You put the key in his jaws, and the gate opens. Now you can go inside. You are now in a chamber lit with torches, at the threshold of the underworld. In the middle of the chamber, there is a huge mirror. You come closer and gaze into the mirror, but it is dormant, and there is no reflection. You reach into another pocket and find a dagger. Cut your hand and let the blood flow onto the mirror. Now it is alive. You can see images moving and changing in it. Gaze into the mirror and observe the visions. All you see is the reflection of your soul - things from your past and your future, subconscious material that you need to explore if you want to grow on the path, your hidden fears, and desires – everything that is buried deep in your personal underworld. When the mirror stops showing images, and the vision fades, leave the chamber, take the key back and go up the stairs back into the woods. Close the working and return to your normal consciousness.

Visions in this working are often accompanied by a lot of Nightside imagery and symbolism. The underworld landscapes are seen both as dark and creepy and enchanting and beautiful. There are pits of fire and sacrificial altars, as well as magic forests with beautiful fountains and waterfalls. Sometimes the entrance leads through labyrinths and endless hallways, old castles and ruins, old forests with gnarly trees and huge cobwebs. Other times, it is hidden among tree branches and rocks. The mirror chamber appears as beautifully ornamented or plain and simple. Sometimes it is a cave, empty or filled with water and lit by torches or candles. Other times, it is a room carved in black crystal, shining and magical, but at the same time simple and dark. The mirror is often a crystal, too - multi-dimensional and fluid, like a living gateway. You may see it shaped like a door or kteis, opening up to consume you and pull you onto the other side. Sometimes it is also seen as made of water - the silvery astral substance that brings associations with the womb of the moon and the amniotic waters of the Lunar Goddess. Many practitioners describe the mirror as a living substance, though, evoking the feeling that something or someone is looking at them from inside or from the other side of the mirror. The image seen in it is always personal for each practitioner and reflects your unconscious material - feelings, emotions, fears, fascinations, ambitions, phobias, fantasies, etc. It is the image of your "Dark Half," the Daimon, often described as the "true original form" as opposed to the illusory image that is seen through the mundane mirror reflections. Many practitioners describe the journey into the underworld as an experience of going inside of themselves, the inner part of the Self, unaware and inaccessible to the mundane Self. Sometimes, also the goddess herself is seen in the mirror, and her form is different than her usual depictions - monstrous and bestial, reflecting her Nightside nature - sometimes with the head of a hound/dog, other times with the face of a wolf or werewolf.

DAY 4
Journey through the Nightside

This meditation is followed by a dream work practice; therefore, it is recommended to perform it shortly before sleep. If possible, you should also sleep in your temple room, within your ritual space.

Follow the same steps as before. Again, sit in a comfortable position and put the sigil in front of you, focusing all your attention on the image. Visualize it glowing and flashing with sparkles of the emerald-green energy of the goddess. At the same time, chant the words of calling:

Hecate Enodia, lead me into the underworld of my soul.
With your dagger, I pierce the veil between life and death!

Like before, keep chanting until you sense the change in the atmosphere in your ritual space and feel ready to continue the working. Drink the sacrament from the chalice and let it fill you with the immortal essence of the goddess. Then close your eyes and continue your visual journey from the point where you left before.

Return to the crossroads in the woods, receive the potion of transformation from the goddess, then go down to the mirror chamber at the threshold of the underworld. This time, envision the goddess with the head of a mare. Again, stand before the mirror. Activate it with your blood and call the name of the goddess. As you gaze at the mirror, at first, you can see your human form in which you came there, but then it changes and morphs. The potion/poison drunk at the crossroads has worked its way through your consciousness to become the elixir of transformation. You are now transforming into a creature of the Nightside. Let it be spontaneous, your new form shaped by your imagination and the energies of the goddess, or you can visualize yourself in a chosen shape. Take as much time as you need for this visualization.

When the transformation is complete, touch the mirror - you will see that it is no longer a solid surface. Now it is silvery, liquid, and three-dimensional, forming a portal to the Nightside from lunar energies of the astral plane, and you can use it as a gate to the labyrinths of the underworld. Ask the goddess to guide you on this journey and step into the mirror. For a moment, all becomes black again, and then the blackness crystallizes and grows into a landscape that you can enter.

Let the vision flow freely and enjoy the experience. When the journey is over, return to your temple and proceed to the dream-working.

DREAM WORK

When the meditation is over, lie down on your bed and bring the image of Hecate's sigil and visions you have just experienced into your mind once again. While gazing at the sigil (you can use the drawn/printed image or simply visualize it in your inner mind), chant the mantra from the first day:

HEKATE TRIMORPHIS TRIODITIS ENODIA

Keep your attention focused on the wish to continue the vision in a dream. If you wake up, focus again on the sigil and try to keep this vision in your mind while falling back asleep. Write down your dreams when you wake up. Take a moment to meditate on whether they are related to the magical work and, if so, how. Do not worry if they seem irrelevant at first, their meaning may be revealed at a later time.

The key motif in this working is transformation into an astral form and traveling through the mirror into the depths of the subconscious. Many practitioners experience here the lupine/lycanthropic energies of the goddess, and the most common vision is transformation into a wolf or werewolf. This is further explored in another working included in this anthology. The wolf is one of Hecate's sacred animals, and the goddess herself has many lupine, predatory aspects that manifest through her witchcraft powers of shape-shifting and astral transformation. Therefore, you can see your image in the mirror as that of a wolf, wolf with wings - bat or dragon wings, grey wolf, black one, half-man half-wolf, werewolf, man with a wolf's face, or beast with yellow-glowing wolf eyes. The lycanthropic transformation is the most common motif here, and other bestial manifestations are rare, although some practitioners see themselves in the form of a snake, dragon, bestial entity with dragon wings or limbs, scorpion or human being with scorpion parts, owl, raven, or spider. The spider manifestation is a common motif as well, usually among female practitioners, pointing at the Arachnid qualities of Hecate's Ophidian current. Other visions of transformation are connected with Hecate's death energies - there are skeletons and vampire beings, black shadows and humanoid entities with red glowing eyes, black dragons, and dark fiery spirits. Sometimes, however, the reflection seen in the mirror is the goddess herself, her essence merged with the consciousness of the practitioner.

The journey through the mirror is always personal and reflects the "dark side" of each practitioner. Some describe it as an immersion in deep, calm, and thick ocean of living darkness. For others, it is entering into a radiant world, bright and shining with light. Some experience the imagery of hell - with volcanic landscapes, sulfurous lakes, black mountains, etc. Others see magic worlds and enchanted mazes. There are also visions of the Void, the living womb of the Dark Goddess of Sitra Ahra, filled with black liquid substance from which the practitioner may create shapes and manifestations of the inner mind.

DAY 5
Invocation of Hecate Trimorphis

Prepare your temple like on the previous day. Pour red wine into the chalice and put it on the altar. Stand or sit in a comfortable position. For a moment, focus on the sigil again and chant the words of calling: *HEKATE TRIMORPHIS TRIODITIS ENODIA,* silently or aloud, in an entrancing rhythm. Feel the energies flowing through the sigil and Hecate's presence behind the gates of the Nightside, awaiting invitation to enter your consciousness. When you feel ready to perform the ritual, begin the invocation.

I invoke Hecate,
The Three-Formed Goddess,
She who has every form and many names,
Guardian of the Dead,
Immortal One,
Daughter of the Night,
Lady of the Crossroads.
I invoke the Mistress of the Three Ways,
She who comes from Darkness into Light,
Shining and beautiful,
Glorious and kind.
I invoke the Lady of the Threshold,
She who cloaks the world with Eternal Night,
Ghastly and terrible,
Cunning and maleficent.
Snake-Girdled One,
Nocturnal One,
Heavenly One,
Blood-drinker and Flesh-eater,
Who devours hearts of those who died untimely,
Who feasts among the graves,
Who comes with hounds and beasts of prey,
With fearsome wolves and venomous snakes,
With howling and hissing,
And in ominous silence.
I invoke the Mistress of All,
Goddess of Darkness and Light,
Born of Primordial Chaos
She who frightens and blesses,
Who holds Cerberus in chains,
And grants the Key to the Gates of the Night.

I call you through your names:

Hecate, Chthonia, Enodia, Antaia, Kourotrophos, Propylaia,
Propolos, Phosphoros, Soteira, Triodia, Trimorphis,
Klêidouchos, Anassa Eneroi, Apotropaia!

Hecate!
Goddess of the Underworld!
Mother of Witchcraft!
Three-Headed Goddess!
Come forth to me!
Lead me through the gates of hell to find the wisdom that lies in the depths.
Let me gaze into the mirror of my soul through your eyes that see everything, deep in the underworld that hides the secret of existence!
Let me taste your transforming poison!
Manifest as the force of my self-creation!

When you finish the words of invocation, drink the sacrament from the chalice. Sit or lie down, and open yourself for energies manifesting in your ritual space and in your consciousness. Let the experience flow freely and spontaneously. Observe the temple and sense phenomena which manifest in the ritual space when the Lady of the Crossroads comes through the gateways of the Night, or close your eyes and let her manifest and speak to you through your inner mind. Even if you do not experience any tangible manifestation or concrete visions, write down all thoughts that you may have after the working and meditate on them for a while, as these might be personal messages from the goddess. Finish the working with the traditional closing:

And so it is done!

Visions of Hecate Trimorphis come with thoughts of death, the underworld, afterlife, passing and being reborn, etc. Change and transformation is necessary in her rites, as well as sacrifice - especially the sacrifice of something personal, a part of ourselves. To travel to the world of the dead, the underworld of the soul, we need to shape-shift and transform our astral bodies into the form of an astral being that will be able to cross the boundaries of worlds. This is a test of courage and balance on the self-initiatory journey into the personal underworld, where we have to face our own death. In Hecate's mirror of the soul, this manifests as a confrontation with our own shadow side, "the Dark Half."

Hecate manifests in this working in several forms. She is a woman in a black hooded dress, holding two candles or torches in her hands. She is a goddess sitting on a dark throne in the middle of the underworld, in a dark chamber or surrounded by nature - forests, marshes, and lakes - accompanied by wolves, dogs, snakes, owls, ravens, and other beasts and spirits of the forest. She is a young woman and a crone, a human being and a predatory beast. She also appears in a stellar form - wearing a crown of stars and moons, walking in astral mist, in a silvery dress reflecting the astral lunar currents. There are visions of fire and flames, pointing at the role of Hecate as the guardian of fire. Some practitioners see her surrounded by flames, while others are faced with fire emanating from her eyes and mouth. She also guards a cauldron filled with a boiling potion. Sensations of Kundalini and the inner fire are often experienced here as well. Sometimes she passes the torch (or torches) to the practitioner so that we can carry the torch and illuminate the way on our journey into the darkness within. Other times, this is about illuminating the way for others. The chalice/cauldron with potion/poison is the elixir of transformation, but also the nectar of knowledge allowing for access to memory and wisdom. It is the poison of the serpent that induces transformation - like the snake shedding its skin, and it is also the intoxicating elixir releasing vital energies of life - the Kundalini force within each human being. It is also the key to the Other Side - like the snake gliding through holes and openings, the Initiate can transform and pass through various layers of the Self on the initiatory journey into the personal underworld through the Crossroads of Hecate. Finally, the fiery energy of the Kundalini serpent is the torch of the goddess, the fire of illumination that lights up the darkness of the soul.

DAY 6
Personal Ritual dedicated to Hecate

The last day concludes the work of the project, and the practices are left to your personal choice. You can repeat the workings from the previous days as a whole, or you can simply open yourself for visions of Hecate's current and let her guide you through the gates of your personal underworld. However, it is recommended to prepare something yourself for this last day - you can write a mantra, meditation, small ritual, design a sigil, draw an image, compose a piece of ritual music, etc. - something inspired by this work and empowered by the energies of the goddess. The ability of self-expression is one of the most important foundations of the Draconian self-initiatory process and all creative efforts are magical operations in themselves.

Make this day personal for you. Take a look at your visions and experiences from the whole project and meditate on your previous and future steps on the path, or your personal relationship with the goddess. Again, you can go to the crossroads or a quiet, desolate place, meditate there and thank the goddess for her presence and guidance. Let this final day be a time of reflections and perhaps new inspirations on your spiritual journey on the Path of the Dragon.

Three Faces of Hecate

Hekate and Heqet

There is not a lot I can say about Hekate that has not been said before, so I won't even bother trying. As many of you know, she is largely considered an Indo-European goddess, adopted by the Greeks, that corresponds to the crossroads, the night, magick, witchcraft, ghosts, necromancy, and sorcery. She also corresponds to herbs, light, and ghosts. Due to her age, she was eventually depicted as a triple goddess, but when put into context of her development, we can see that it is a small part of her character. Yes, of course, she responds if you call her this way, but contextually speaking, this is not a strong correspondence. She is usually seen as holding two keys or torches, and in modern artwork, both can generally be found on images and statuary of her. An interesting point to note, though, is that even though she was considered one of the household gods in ancient Greece, being in the spotlight like that was not something that usually went along with her character, as you can probably deduce from the first list of correspondences. In that way, because she was "grandfathered in" (as the corporate saying goes) to the Greek pantheon, she was never really on the same level or seen as part and parcel to any of the other Greek gods. Since she is most likely older than all of the other Greek gods, her origins are shrouded in mystery from an archaeological perspective, and many theories exist on where she comes from and when.

One of those theories, the one that is the most plausible, is that she was originally Egyptian. In the writings of Kenneth Grant, he explores the connection between her and an ancient Egyptian goddess named "Heqet." After all, both were connected with the frog, and the syllables are related, so of course, they are. This is an interesting lesson in archaeolinguistics. Just because two words are spelled similarly and may even sound the same, they do not have to be related. An excellent example of this that I have written elsewhere about is the name Anubis and the country of Nubia. They look related on the surface, but when you do your research, you find they are not. Yes, ancient Nubia bordered Egypt, and they have been historically known as enemies, but Anubis is the Greek word for the Egyptian word Anpu, which is the actual name. There is no evidence that Anpu came from Nubia or was connected to Nubia in ancient times. We have to watch out for mental pitfalls like this because if we are not mindful, we may find ourselves going down rabbit holes that are psychologically dangerous and wasteful. Thorough research is necessary. When I was reading Grant's material, I thought that was profound, but now that I am older, more knowledgeable, and have had time to digest it, I still find it an interesting theory, but I am not sure of its truth. A growing voice says that they are not related and that Hekate originally came from the Anatolians. But then again, some people say she is one hundred percent Greek. So really, no one knows, and these are all theories. Because of the material in Grant, though, and how much it is fundamental material to the Western Esoteric Tradition, it does deserve a discussion.

And that is the point of this essay. I will share information for you to make an informed decision on where you think she originated. After all, the way you work with her is unique to your path, thus making it highly subjective. In this case, subjective equates with malleable. For the next oh-so, however many long words, I will compare the two, Hekate and Heqet, so you can decide for yourself whether or not the two are connected. This should save you a lot of time in your studies so that you can apply that extra time to doing the work, rather than reading about it. A harmony between reading and doing should be maintained in order to fully enjoy the world, which we are all here to do in our ways. To clarify even further, there will be a chart to use!

First, let's look at their ages. Technically, and this is really splitting hairs, Heqet is older. But then again, the ancient Egyptian culture was older than ancient Greek, so this is not surprising at all. Heqet, the wife of Amun, dates back to approximately 3200 BCE, whereas, in a liberal sense, the Greek gods were not really worshipped as a system until 3000 BCE. If you subscribe to the theory that she was Indo-European, then this would make her older than that, putting her in range of the ancient Egyptian deities. But then again, by the time of Heqet being known as the wife of Amun, she would have had to have been around for quite some time, which would still make her older. It is interesting to think about this, though, because almost no matter how you justify it, they are around the same age. So in this way, they could be related, but probably not the same deity transcribed onto the other.

This last fact is because of their correspondences. I listed some of hers above, but let's put them into the correspondences for Heqet and see if and how they match up.

Hekate	Heqet
Crossroads	Fertility
The Night	Breathed life into the body at birth (midwifery)
Magick	The later stages of childbirth (midwifery)
Witchcraft	The flooding of the Nile
Ghosts	Magick
Necromancy	Medicine
Sorcery	Magical Energy
Herbs	
Light	
Later, a triple goddess	

The correspondences in brackets are an interesting point to consider. The term "midwifery" above is placed there because both of those functions occur on the midwife's watch, and a common association for Heqet is midwifery, one that is lacking in Hekate. But, the three terms in brackets come from the Egyptian god Heka. This is not generally looked at when analyzing Hekate, but it should be looked at in-depth. The main difference between Heka and Hekate, though, is that Heka is a god, and Hekate is a goddess, whereas Heqet is a goddess, as Hekate. The list above is an amalgamation of the two Egyptian deities. I do this because the majority of the time, people are looking at this material from a black and white, right or wrong, duality perspective. As Aleister Crowley has pointed out repeatedly, if you're looking at things from that perspective, you are not stepping back and looking at the whole picture. I agree with this and have found it true more often than not. What if, instead of Hekate coming from Heqet, she came from a blend of Heka and Heqet? It is entirely plausible. It is pretty likely, too, but that is my opinion showing. I do not believe in coincidence, though, and thus I do firmly believe there is some connection happening here between Hekate and ancient Egypt. But as to what extent, I do not know. There are so many differences between the two that it does cast serious doubt on the connection between them. But a lot of the essence between the three is common, fertile ground, so it cannot be discounted carte blanche, either. Making the subject more obtuse is the fact that the Egyptian word Heka not only means a god; it also means "magick" in general. And even that is not quite right because it means magical energy as much as it means the skill set of magick. This ambiguousness does serve to connect the three beings we have been discussing, though.

Consider this. Several of Hekate's correspondences could fall under this blanket term and concept, and we should take this into account when analyzing this subject. Witchcraft, necromancy, sorcery, and magick could all be classified under the auspice of the Egyptian god Heka since Heka is magick, and witchcraft, sorcery, and necromancy are all forms of magick. In this way, we could condense things down for a shorter list:

Hekate	Heqet/Heka
Crossroads	Midwifery
The Night	Fertility/Nile Inundation
Magick	Magick
Herbs	Medicine
Light	Magical Rituals

I separate magical rituals from magick in the correspondence list for Heqet/Heka because, in ancient Egypt, it was believed that all was magick, and magick was all. There was no division between mundane life and magical life, or everyday practices and magical practices. Heka was as common and active as oxygen. Let's break it down into a compare and contrast analysis.

First, the Crossroads/Midwifery point. Really, these are the same, but they are different, right? At the late stage of childbirth, the soul and body are just about the exact point of the crossroads, half in, half out, so we can see a parallel here. A lot of people make a mistake when working with her to think that this only means a physical crossroad, but it most certainly does not. A crossroads is a juncture. It is, in a substantial way, a twilight point. It is that point after, but before at the same time, and the opportunities and possibilities are almost endless. Performing the function of being a midwife is straddling the two worlds, too, in many ways. I have noticed this from many professional midwives that I have known over the years. As much as you are trained on the biological and physical side, there is also the psychological component learned. This is also the time of Anpu, Ianus, and any other deity that is "half in, half out."

When we move down the list to the next point, things get thrown for a loop - the night vs midwifery. Well, let's remember some basic ideas here to clarify. Remember, it is a common practice for a new, conquering religion to demonize the older, established religion. If you keep that in mind, you can see that potentially, the traits of Hekate having to do with witchcraft and necromancy could be traits ascribed to her in a demonization way and goal. In that way, it becomes clear how one is the inverse of the other. I'm not saying that is true now because I know many witches that correspond to fertility just as easily as they do to necromancy. I mean, in a classical sense, fertility and necromancy would have been seen as polar opposites. But of course, Heqet would still have been quite respected and powerful, so in this particular case, you couldn't just get rid of all of the positive traits of Heqet. You would have had to leave some for the worshippers to stick with as you gradually influenced society. Following this line of logic, the rest of the correspondences become clear when you stop to think about them. For example, herbs would lead to medicine, and through magical rituals, light, true light, would be produced. And, remember that both identify with the frog! Hail the frog!

So, the main question proposed here is, what if Hekate is a descendant of Heqet and a corruption of her? You can see how that is one possibility. However, this does not look at the Anatolian roots, so let us turn our attention there. This is a short conversation, though, as everything is summed up in scientific dating. The conservative time for the Anatolians is approximately 1350 BCE. When we plug that into our equations, we see that even if we add another thousand years, it is still the most recent of any time periods listed. Therefore while yes, Hekate may have strong Anatolian influences, these are much later in the development of her character. Therefore, while she may have been defined through the Anatolian system, she existed for centuries, if not a thousand years before.

There is something particular of note here, which is the connection between the Anatolians and the Minoans. When we speak of the Anatolians, we speak of an area, and within that area are different groups of people. One of the groups of people were known as the "Carians," and it is from them that it is believed Hekate originated. But, and this is the key point for those of you that look at Hekate as having Atlantean ties, it is believed that the Carians were the precursors to the Minoans!

Why is that relevant, you ask? One of the standard and well-supported theories is that the Minoans were the Atlanteans. While this is highly debated and almost wild speculation, it is worth considering none the less. Philosophically, things do line up, but geologically they do not, which is worth keeping in mind when you look at these stories. Regarding Hekate, though, this is an interesting point to consider because when you think about it, this means that either Hekate was A) Egyptian in origin, B) Atlantean in original (through the above logic), or C) Greek. Really, I don't subscribe to the Greek theory, but I will admit my bias because of my interest and experience with ancient Egypt. The Greeks are watered down Egyptian mixed with a splash of Persia, and that's about it. That leaves us with either Anatolian or Egyptian and I think it was a blending of the two.

Here is my take away on it, and after you read it, ponder your own. I believe that she was Egyptian in creation but was demonized by the later Anatolians, which became mythicized as the Atlanteans, which eventually made its way to the Greeks. Does this mean that I think the Minoans were the Atlanteans? For the sake of this essay, yes. But, in my paradigm, no, not at all. Geology tells us the Atlantean story was much earlier than that, and I prefer to go with facts. So while I believe the Minoans were not the Atlanteans, in the context of Hekate, this conversation does explain the often cited (but usually incorrect) connection with Hekate to Atlantis rather than Egypt. However, this also means that there is credence given to the connection between Hekate, Heqet, and Heka. So, who is she to you? Where do you think she originates? And most importantly, does it matter? Whether you use some of the correspondences listed above for her, or all of them, the fact of the matter remains that she is mysterious, alluring, and powerful. In a lot of ways, she is very much like the stories of the Nephilim from other areas of the world, but that is a conversation for another time.

DENERAH ERZEBET

Spiritual Alchemy of the Triple Goddess

In its current phase, the Typhonian Tradition employs pre-Christian deities in their archetypal rather than literal embodiment. This involves unveiling the psycho-sexual mechanism at the heart of all subsequent entification, whether through mythical narrative or aesthetic representation. As such, our work involves a backward process, wherein personal attributes such as gender, behavior, and spiritual power are keys to uncovering the primal function of any god or goddess.

In fact, the three qualities of Gender, Behavior/Personality, and Spiritual Power/Authority form a triple-essence through which the Typhonian Magician can become a god or goddess through practical use of the sex-magick formula concealed therein. As such, Typhonian magick doesn't involve a revival of polytheistic worship, but rather the unveiling of the True Self or Hidden God through the psychopomp glyphed as one's deity.

However, an exclusive invocation of a singular deity is not enough to become magically-proficient. One must also acquire deep familiarity with an entire pantheon to properly-understand the specific role of one's deity therein. This is because gender manifests as male-female polarity, both requiring one another to fully-understand themselves.

Thus, the goddess-worshipper must know her male consort(s) and accounts of their interactions (behavior) to command these natural forces toward serving her Will. Thus, the "god-seeker" must know their mythical allies and enemies, as well as their own "natural office" (what the deity represents/presides over), to take full advantage of this divine authority.

Such is the premise employed in the present unveiling of Hecate, primarily-known as the triple goddess of the Moon, Witchcraft, and the three stages of Womanhood (i.e., Maiden, Mother/Wife, and Crone).

Obviously, my inquiry is archetypal rather than personal. Thus, Hecate's lunar association is equated with archetypal Womanhood as the passive gender. This, in turn, is subdivided into the three fundamental aspects of spiritual alchemy or initiation (i.e., witchcraft). As such, each face corresponds to the following concepts:

1) The Maiden embodies the eternal, pure self, often called Daimon or Holy Guardian Angel.
2) The Crone represents the Shadow or shades of acquired personality.
3) The Mother is the Magician himself or herself, the mediator between light and shadow, capable of birthing new worlds.

As will become clear throughout this essay, these female depictions are universally-applicable, regardless of the Magician's physical gender.

1.
THE MAIDEN

Hecate's maiden or virgin aspect embodies spiritual, rather than sexual, innocence. In this case, innocence toward the human condition is not ignorance thereof, as many would assume. Most children exhibit vivid imagination and sharp insight on deep metaphysical "facts," even if they can't express them with the same skill acquired by a university graduate. Instead, they use art forms to express themselves, which still get the point across despite their "crude" appearance.

In fact, any criticism of crudeness (whether linguistic or artistic) emerges from culturally-conditioned adults who have been groomed via education to become functional within a limited paradigm. Not only have we been taught how to "act properly," but we were also urged to "think properly"- as if external behavior (merely a practical necessity) wasn't enough!

In magical terms, refined intellectual and literary skills are obviously necessary to decipher texts and myths written by adults. However, when one is asked to draw their own sigils, craft implements, or write an invocation, self-doubt arises due to a programmed obsession to "do it right." This also carries into the ritual itself, where one questions if their results were "legitimate," whether this concerns gnosis, visions, manifestations, etc.

This self-doubt is absent in young children. They paint, draw, sing, and dance in harmony with pure and direct insight, many of their drawings resembling sigils or alien gateways, while song and dance evoke impressions of ancient shamanic rites.

This is the fearless innocence or pure selfhood of one's divine potential. Depending on what path you follow, this is often referred to as Higher Self, Daimon, Augoeides, or Holy Guardian Angel.

Before moving on to the next aspect, I'd like to make a brief remark on the role of erotic pleasure within the context of daimonic innocence. Many practitioners maintain a very erotic relationship with their Daimon or personal deity. However, this is erotic rather than the scientifically-confined notion of sexuality. Rather than relegate itself to rationalization, the love between Magician and Daimon goes beyond biology, ethics, and sexual orientation.

To experience "innocent love," one must confront the Shadow, embodying the lingering inhibitions instilled by experiential conditioning.

2.
THE CRONE

Symbolically, the old age typified by the Crone or sterile woman makes more sense if we describe her aspect as "maturity" or the process of maturing itself. As such, the Crone embodies a process of forcibly-distancing oneself from innocence, relinquishing the magical universe in favor of sterile realism. While some social customs are necessary for practical survival (i.e. financial ambition), many are just by-products of religious conservatism and patriarchal bias.

Of course, everyone experiences these values in varying degrees, depending on how traditional one's role-models may have been. We must also consider exceptional cases wherein shadow-complexes were spawned by severe emotional and physical trauma. Generally, victims of sexual assault, manipulation, or severe punishment acquire complexes in their most extreme and obscuring form.

Mainstream media portrays these veils in the form of "demonic possession." Typically, the possessed is a recently-traumatized individual who equates reality with their shadow-complex, unintentionally-inviting Qliphothic energies when the daimonic light is severely-obscured. Additionally, many survivors turn to drugs, alcohol, or self-harm to cope, these destructive habits reinforcing the influence of sinister forces.

Of course, possession is less common than obsession. The former is the furthest point in a gradual process where the invading entity assumes total control of a body after all personal defenses have been erased. Obsession is the process itself, which rarely-culminates toward total-possession. We are all obsessed in varying degrees, depending on our upbringing and experiences. Just as we all carry the maiden; we also collect shadows.

Many shadows, despite being acquired, are relatively harmless. These include organizational habits, personal routines, speech patterns, and mannerisms, to name a few. Those directly-affecting the personality can also be seen as extensions of the daimonic will or defense mechanisms serving to ground and protect this childlike whimsy. Such personality-shades are likely born from positive encounters, both platonic and sexual.

In fact, the relationship between Maiden and Crone builds itself around cooperation and mutual benefit. The Daimon requires reality-shades to accomplish its purpose in a rational and materialistic society, whether as magical servitors or astral guards. In exchange, shadows receive the nourishing spirit-energy of daimonic consciousness, without which they cannot thrive as self-sufficient entities.

All this takes place through the mediating mind of the Magicians themselves. This is the Mother-Matrix of all manifestation, the central nexus of the magical universe.

3.

THE MOTHER

The truly-realized Magician, partaking of both eternal and temporal identities, isn't an identity as such but a dynamic vessel constantly-renewing and adapting itself to various phenomenal conditions. In this sense, Daimon and Shadows are simultaneously manipulated throughout one's incarnated existence. Ceremonial magick offers a practical example through the standard procedure of banishing, purification, invocation, consecration, and evocation.

First, all shades are banished and the ritual space purified so that the Daimon can manifest upon a blank slate in both an external and internal sense. After the Daimon has been invoked, the Magician is consecrated therewith, granting them the spiritual authority necessary to command the shadows. These are evoked one by one, wherein the useless shades are permanently exorcised and useful ones constrained to serve the Daimonic Self.

The example above is, obviously, a later stage in one's spiritual development. At first, the Magician should stick with banishing/purification and simply invoking the Daimon for divination or meditation purposes. Only once a firm grasp of the "true self" is obtained can one proceed with exorcism and binding. Typically, "knowledge and conversation" with the Daimon occupies several years, during which the Magician is informed regarding which shades ought to be removed and which carry creative potential.

Rather than give a mere summary, I decided to conclude this essay by offering two ritual pathworkings opening onto a deeper understanding of the Daimon/Shadow relationship. Pathworking, or a guided meditation, is a common method used in Left-Hand-Path traditions for personal transformation. As such, they provide an effective gateway for deep exploration of the subconscious mind.

4.

PATHWORKING:
WHERE LIGHT AND SHADOW MEET

First Pathworking:

Use a banishing ritual you're familiar with and can perform with effectiveness. After you've cleared the ritual space, take a few moments to relax through a meditation technique of your choice, followed by an energy raising procedure (several methods are included in Asenath Mason's *Draconian Ritual Book*).

When you feel ready, visualize the Daimon to your left and a shadow-form to your right. If your Daimon typically appears as female, then the shadow must be given a male form or vice-versa. If you don't know your Daimon, then project a pleasing form reminding you of pure joy and unrestrained whimsy (fairy, nymph, or winged human creatures are recommended). The shadow will take the anthropomorphic image of an acquired belief.

Visualize both entities having sex. At the moment of orgasm, see them melt and merge into the form of a pregnant woman in royal clothing (I suggest red or purple robes with gold jewelry). She then gives birth to a refined version of you, harmonizing both daimonic and shadow consciousness.

Think of leaving your ritual space as being reborn from the womb of the Mother, capable of achieving your daily goals with absolute confidence.

Second Pathworking:

Prepare the ritual space with banishings and energy raising methods, as prescribed in the previous pathworking.

Regardless of gender or sexual orientation,* assume the form of a female shadow. Your Daimon, for this rite, will take the active male role. Lie down as you watch the Daimon penetrate you, loving you passionately.

He injects you with his purifying seed, and suddenly you become brighter, cleansed of previous shadow energy.

Give thanks for this consecration, and close the ritual.

* Erotic pleasure is not the purpose of this rite, so the instructions apply to everyone. The sex involved therein is technical, using polarity for the sake of spiritual transformation.

Tree of Death

KEONA KAI'NATHERA

Hecate Workings

We all know the history, lore, and myth concerning Hecate/Hekate, so I am not going to bombard you with information that I am sure you already know. Let's begin.

Hecate's workings will "need" the following items:

- Flying ointment tincture or balm
- A small basin full of water with mint oil added to it, and ice* (if you can take the coldness)
- Towels to put under the basin
- A chair for sitting
- Lancet
- Hecate's sigil on a purple background, drawn in black marker
- One large black candle
- One large purple candle
- Incense of choice. For me, Jasmine was called for, but use what you wish.
- Grape based wine with mint added, or grape juice*
- Crescent-shaped bread made with cheese and garlic*
- Moon meal*

The items with an * next to them are optional. You do not need physical food. You can have an offering of whatever type you wish. I used these items as they are Hecate's, and it was what

I personally wanted to do. My moon meal was pasta and alfredo sauce with garlic bread. All made while reciting her enn.

In these meditations and workings, you will be given a few keys from Hecate. Each key leads to a different door of your own construct that she has provided for you.

DAY 1

Ground yourself, raise your Draconian energy, and connect to the Temple.* See the members walking around and talking with one another. Note the statues of the gods, the smell of the incense in the air. Feel the blood racing through your veins. Become the Dragon and soar. Head toward the Temple's door, focusing on the symbol.

Once at the door, push open the gates and walk through them. Come back to your astral form and prepare yourself for this journey. To your left, there are items on the table specific to your journey. Change into the clothing, go to the door with Hecate's sigil on it,† and sit down in the lotus position.

Hecate is leading you on a walk through the underworld. You will work through a multitude of issues that you have carried with you up until now. Hecate will not make it easy for you, and you will face issues that you may have thought long gone or that you had conquered. Be prepared spiritually, mentally, and emotionally.

Center your thought on Hecate's sigil, the darkness of the underworld, the smell of the caves. Light the black and purple

---

* If you are not a temple member, you can connect to any Hecate worship paradigm that you find personally appealing.
† The recommended sigil is the one from page 13.

candles, and ignite your incense. Add a drop of blood to her sigil.

Close your eyes, and wait for Hecate to give you the key so you can unlock the gate. Once through, Hecate will guide you to another aspect of herself. Take heed to what she is telling you. Once you have reached your destination, she will appear to you in a familiar fashion. Take her hand, and notice how it feels in yours. For the rest of the journey, you are walking with her. Face your fears, let the energy of the underworld take you deep into your subconscious. Be one with it, do not be afraid of what is there. Meet it head-on. Listen to the advice she shares with you, watch what she does, pay close attention to her.

Once you are finished, you will be returned to the gate where Hecate will be in her original form. She reaches out to you. You bid the other Hecate goodbye and step through the gate. Again, listen to those departing words, feelings, or signs that you are being given. After you are back on the other side of the gate, bid Hecate goodbye and lock the gate.

Slowly open your eyes and awaken. Start moving your body from the toes up. Thank Hecate, for her time and wisdom.

Make sure you write down everything as you unwind.

DAY 2
Hecate as Leviathan:
The Triple Water of Emotional Chaos

Connect to Hecate as you did on Day 1. Light your candles, your incense, and drop blood onto her sigil. For this working use the sigil provided on the next page.

Here you will fill your small basin with ice (if want) and water. Add some mint essential oil or mint-like oil, peppermint can work, and so can eucalyptus. You can use mint leaves or dried mint if you have no oil.

Sit in your chair, and add a cushion if you need it. You may be sitting for a while. Place your bare feet in the basin of water. Continue your connection to Hecate. Once you have connected, open the gate with your key and enter. Deep within, the storm is reaching its intensity. You are in the middle of the waters; nothing but blackness surrounds you. You feel the waves hitting and crashing into you at all angles. You hear the thunder. It cracks to your left, then your right, then inside of you. The pain is sharp. You grab your chest. You hear the barking of hounds off in the distance, but you feel the wind from their bark. You turn to run, but it is too late. With your first step, you fall beneath the first wave.

Water fills your lungs. You're grasping for air, clawing your way through the frigid waters to reach the surface. You're fighting a losing battle. You slow your strokes and see bubbles escaping from your nose and mouth. You hear and feel the crack of your chest as your lungs cave in, causing you to release one final breath of air. You're sinking. She touches your hand. She pulls you to her. Accept what she is giving you. She smiles and disappears. Something is wrapped around your left ankle, and it's pulling you down to the second wave.

Beautiful blackness. Poisonous breathing. Slick and velvet looking creatures. They are all around you. To your right, you have a curious friend. Follow them to the cave. On your way, you see remnants of others who didn't accept her gift, others who are struggling for breath, begging for your help. You know you cannot help them, as each path is personal. All choices and decisions you make and take are your own. The waters feel warmer, yet they can't be as you go deeper below the dark skies and raging storm. You are in the cave now. Your friend has something for you. What is it? Go deeper in, toward the door, and find out. Once the door is open, you see he's waiting for you. He reaches out to you. Take what is given to you. His beautiful blue skin shines intensely in the flashes of light. He whispers to you...something you should always have and where to get it. As you swim with him, the current picks up. Moving at a fantastic speed, you struggle to match his pace. Minutes later, you find yourself approaching the third wave. Place the gift Hecate gave you, the item you received in the cave, and what he told you to get and place them within the circle. When you step back, what do you see? Take your time and focus on what is in front of you. Record everything you see, hear, feel, and sense.

When you are finished, you move backward and fall through the waters. They are coming toward you. A beautiful woman with blue skin, dark hair, and knowing eyes; surrounded by serpents of the sea. One that is significantly larger has deep blue eyes and is breathing fire. As they are getting closer, they merge into one. Moving faster, He opens his mouth, and you feel this unbearable, sharp pain.

You emerge from the waters, blood dripping from your right arm, your breathing is shallow, eyes are dilated. The storm subsides as you walk across the waters. You have a purpose in your step. You look up and out in front of you, heading to that door with the long, deep, and sharp black cracks in it. Behind you, they walk, slowly following your every step.

Come back to consciousness slowly. When you are all the way out, remove your feet from the water. Dry your feet and record your session.

DAY 3
Journey to Hecate

Here you will need wine and food offerings. Start your meditation the same as previous days with the candles, incense, blood, and sigil (from Day 1).

You are no longer in your present realm. You are walking toward a large black door. There are cracks all through it, and it looks as though if you touch it, it will break apart. The path in front of you is bare; soft dirt is at your feet. The trees are black and fragile but full of leaves. You look up and notice that the purple sky is dotted with stars. You see a large orange planet to your right. It looks like it is about to hit the planet you are standing on. It has dark orange lines and white lines with a black crescent shape to the left. You notice similar planets of assorted sizes and colors as well. All are giving off their own energy. Dark green, pale blue, white, and red. Some with rings, others with what looks like waves.

As you approach the door, it moves to let you continue down the path. When you look ahead, you see her. Flowing black robes blowing, even though there is no wind. Mahogany brown hair is clouding her face, but those eyes are piercing. It's Her.

She turns and proceeds down the path. You follow her, taking in all the scenery. The trees, the countless dogs, the grass, the feel of the sun on you, even though no sun is present. Bats, snakes, and toads are everywhere. You are joined by one of her animals. What is it? What are they telling you? What have you been given?

Looking up, she is right in front of you. Her hand is out. Do you take it? After a moment of hesitation, you reach and grasp her hand. It is soft, warm, firm. She seems to fade away, and when you look at your hand, you are, too. Fall into her arms, and she is there to catch you, to guide you. You close your eyes, feel your feet leave the ground. Stay in the moment until she brings you back. Open your eyes. Record what you see.

Here you will present your offerings that you made or brought for Hecate. Even if you chose not to offer food, that is ok. Lay everything you have out in front of you. Grab your incense and light it along with the candles and the usual blood offering on her sigil. Go into a light trance, chanting Hecate's enn* of your own design. Let the smell and wine transport you to the goddess herself. Take your time on your journey. Write down everything you encounter and all your sensations. Thoughts, visions, smells, feels, anything you note. Come back when you are ready and have a meal with Hecate, looking back over what you just wrote.

After your meal has finished, go back to the door at the beginning of the meditation. There she will give you a key. Take the key from her and unlock the door. The door shatters like glass and is hurling pieces at you, but it stops, and through the floating shards of wood, you see her eyes and notice that there are wheels turning in them. After what seems like hours,

---

* An enn is a sentence or group of words in an unknown, "mysterious" or "otherworldly" language. Enns are usually channeled by practitioners and can be found in various books and online resources. If you don't have your own "enn" to recite, replace it with a mantra, such as e.g. "Hekate, Trimorphis, Trioditis, Enodia."

you turn your attention toward the shards and realize you are in a bright field with a dark blue tree, carrying purple leaves and a black bench. She is waiting for you. Go sit next to her and wait. Come back to consciousness when you are ready.

DAY 4
Hecate's Shadow Wheel:
Invocation and Dream Work

Hecate, Blackness of the Crossroads. Proceed as you do every time with the raising of energies and setting up. Take three deep breaths, call out to Hecate, saying:

Hecate I invoke you, align me with the Void.
Hecate, I fully walk into the Blackness of your Soul.

You awaken to see her in front of you. Her black skin looks like the Void itself has taken shape, and her black hair dances with the stars, making it seem like the universe is flowing from her headband. She turns her back to you, and as she steps off, she shapeshifts into a cat. What type of cat do you see? Follow the cat up the path toward the tree. Take note of what is around you. The cat shifts into a snake (what type of snake do you see?) and slithers into the base of the tree. You stop and drop down on both knees. You see something glimmering inside of the tree. You reach in and feel a prick. You snatch your hand back and see the blood fall from your hand. A spider runs out. What type of spider is it? It runs up your clothes and enters your left ear. What are you feeling, what do you see? The spider drops back out of your ear, and you fall back onto mossy grass. The smell is earthy, musky, and intoxicating. When your eyes finally open, you note that the world looks different. You shapeshifted into your astral animal and feel yourself being lifted. She is holding you in her hands. Look into her eyes. Make that connection to her, and record what you see and feel.

She sits you back down, and you turn back into yourself. Standing up, you see her smiling at you. She beckons you to sink to both knees. As you lower your head, you feel a numbing sensation and the tug of your head. You see black sludge dropping next to you. She is removing all the fear that you have. When you entered the Void, you opened yourself up to the Blackness of your soul. You are ready to release your fears, ready to move forward. Let all your fears go, show them to her and conquer them. After you are comfortable with all that you wanted to be released, stand up. Take what she gives you and let it be a reminder to not let your fear control your life. She walks you around the tree, but there is a ravine in front of you. You turn to look at her. She grabs you, kisses your forehead, and throws you into the ravine.

Gently come to, and prep for bed as the next part is a dream working.

Once you are ready for bed, go back to that moment of being thrown into the ravine. You land on a mound of dirt. It is so soft that when you try to get up, you just sink deeper in it. Unable to keep your balance, you give up. Notice the smell of the ravine, similar to mandrake and mint. Close your eyes and chant:

Lady of the Shapeshifting Void
As I drift into the Darkness
I follow your path to the Lunar Dark
Bless me as I move on to the three paths of the underworld.

Record your vision in your dream journal when you wake up.

DAY 5
3 Paths of Learning

Go back to the ravine using the previous day's methods. You crawl out of the dirt, leaving that part of you behind. When you look back, the ravine is full of black gunk. Snap your fingers and set it on fire. To stay on track, you drink the elixir of the underworld that appears in your hand. Wander the earth until you find the three paths of Hecate. Step where the paths intersect. In her hands are three keys, each representing a path you must walk down and unlock to understand yourself better.

She gives you all three keys and hands you her elixir. You are to take three sips on each path at various times on the path. The first sip is taken at the beginning of the path, the second sip at the middle, and the last sip at the end. Light the incense, offer up a drop of blood, and recite Hecate's enn x9. Then proceed onto the paths.

The first path is where you will restore your spiritual body, reconstructing it. You will cleanse and connect with your spiritual self a little deeper than normal. The second path is working on your mental reconstruction. Remove all mental blockages from your mind. Your final path is made of tar, where you will have all your trials, issues, and deeply embedded hurt ripped from your body as you traverse this path. Walking down this path, you feel the tar getting stickier and stickier. Do not stop; keep drudging through until you are at the end of the path. These paths may be down in three days or doing one a day.

After you have finished the paths, walk back through the door on your last path and come back to your body, slowly. Record all that you have gone through.

DAY 6
The Final Gate

Set yourself up as the previous day's workings. Call on Hecate, and you will receive another set of 3 keys that will help you purge any residuals from the last working if you find yourself feeling heavy again. This can be done at any time by recalling the key and re-walking the path.

You have spent the past few days walking with the many forms of Hecate. You have uncovered hurt, pain, confusion, and new-found life. You have walked down paths that have tested your patience, gotten rid of insecurities you thought were deeply gone and removed. You have done a lot of self-work on yourself to get to this point. Beyond the gate is the ending of your physical journey and the beginning of your spiritual one with Hecate and your higher self.

Offer her some food and drink, then recite:

I am ready to move beyond the Gate
I have conquered the faults that needed to be released
I have allowed myself to be stripped bare of my own doubts and
issues from deep within
I offer these gifts to you for helping me reach these points
Your strength and guidance were and will continue to be a
blessing in my life
I give myself to you, and I am our daughter/son.

Focus on the response and visions and sensations that you are being shown. Afterward, enjoy the silence between you as you connect with the goddess on a personal level. When you are ready, follow her to the Gate. Walk through the Gate and return to your body, slowly.

DAY 7
Reflection and Rest

At this point, you have traversed a great many paths and have lightened your spiritual, mental, and emotional self greatly. Your path is a lot clearer than it was seven days ago. Use all that was given to you to reflect on how you will move forward.

The Torch Bearer

Hecate - Guide to the Underworld

This working is an invocation of Hecate in her psychopomp aspect, followed by a pathworking centered on the descent into the underworld with the goddess as a guide. The purpose of the journey is to commune with your ancestors, deceased loved ones, or simply shades of the dead residing behind the veil of life and death. Hecate's role as a guide to the underworld is derived e.g. from the myth of Persephone. In the Homeric Hymn to Demeter, Hecate is the only one who hears Persephone's cries after she is abducted by Hades and held in his dark kingdom. She descends to the underworld to assist Persephone in the journey between the world of the living and the dead and to light up the way with her torches. Hecate also comes to share Demeter's joy when the goddess is eventually reunited with her daughter.

For the ritual itself, you will need several things. First of all, prepare eleven back candles, put them in the circle, and stand or sit inside it. For the ritual, you will also need a dagger or knife, a tool to draw blood (if it is something else), and the sigil of Hecate included on page 13 as a gateway to her current. Perhaps during the journey into the underworld the goddess will reveal a symbol that will be meant just for you, but in the initial contact with her use the one provided here. You may also burn some incense on charcoal during the ritual – the recommended fragrance is either myrrh or rosemary. Feel free to decorate your altar for this working as you want – with statues or images of the goddess, dried flowers and herbs, skulls and death imagery, and anything else you think might be suitable to create a proper ritual space for the goddess to manifest.

Another thing that we will use in this work is the so-called Hecate's Supper. Traditionally, it was a meal served to the goddess and her retinue of spirits on the dark of the moon or the last night of the lunar month. It was left at the crossroads or in front of the home between public and private space. Traditional food for Hecate's Supper included eggs, fish, goat and sheep cheese, sprats, red mullet, garlic, mushrooms, and honey cake. Sometimes it was surrounded by blazing torches or cakes decorated with candles. Place it all on your altar, and after the ritual, take the offerings and leave them in front of your house. Ideally, they should be left at the point of three crossing roads, but any kind of crossing paths or a place signifying a "threshold," like a gate, door, etc., will also work well for this ritual.

The psychopomp in mythology and literature is a spirit or deity that helps the soul of the deceased cross over between the world of man and the realm of the dead. The word itself derives from Greek and translates to "the guide of souls." Therefore, the psychopomp is a being that itself exists in between the worlds and can move freely across the border that separates the realm of the living and the dead, or in magic. This may be symbolic of crossing the barrier between waking and sleeping. This can also refer to liminal trances in which consciousness is suspended between the waking world and the dreaming reality and can explore both, like in the case of astral travel or lucid dreaming. Hecate is both a psychopomp and a liminal goddess - liminal meaning standing at the threshold of the worlds, herself belonging to none, and thus capable of opening all kinds of gateways for the Initiate to travel through them. She is, therefore, a powerful embodiment of this archetype. This is also connected with her role as the

Lady of the Crossroads. The crossroads in mythologies is a symbol of the meeting point between realms and dimensions. It is here that the underworld, the middle world (the world of man), and the realm of the spirits meet and intersect, and it is from here that the practitioner can set out on a journey to the Other Side.

The Crossroads of Hecate is the meeting point of the worlds. Here she appears as the queen of heaven, hell, and earth, and here manifest her powers connected with the dead, death, and resurrection. She is associated with many goddesses, such as Hel - the Queen of the Dead, Gullveigr - the guardian of Divine Knowledge, or the Fates who weave the web of destinies linking each life and soul in the universe. Her powers are those of transformation - dying and being reborn through various rites of passage, including death itself. She appears as a guide and initiator - psychopomp leading souls through three worlds - the land of the dead in the underworld, the world of man on earth, and the world above, the empyrean realm. Her powers open the way between worlds and dimensions - that is why one of her main symbols is the key. Invoking her essence into the practitioner's mind opens the way to all these worlds, making the Initiate a living manifestation of her crossroads, allowing for the descent and the ascent through the axis of the universe.

The following invocation is used in the Temple of Ascending Flame to establish the initial contact with Hecate as the initiatrix and guide on the path to Sitra Ahra. It includes an incantation derived from "The Cry of the 27th Aethyr" in *The Vision and the Voice* by Aleister Crowley. The sigil has been received and earthed through my work with Hecate and is also used within the Temple as the primary sigil of the goddess. The meditation involves a concept of a journey through the veil of life and death to meet your ancestors and to explore your ancestral power and heritage.

The best time to perform this ritual is on Samhain, i.e. October 31st or All Hallows Day (November 1st). Traditionally, this was the time when the veil between the realm of the living and the dead was believed to be the thinnest and when people could summon their ancestors and commune with them through works of necromancy. In European folklore, All Hallows Day and the days before and after were believed to be the time when unquiet souls rose from their graves to haunt the living or to seek help if they could not rest. During that time, they could be evoked by a necromancer, who communicated with them, either for his own benefit or as a service performed to the community, obtaining knowledge of the Other Side and helping them cross over and find peace. In modern times, Samhain can still be used as a liminal time in rites of magic, especially in works of necromancy, to summon discarnate souls from behind the veil or to travel to the underworld in search of knowledge and power that the dead may hold. The ideal place to perform it is a desolate spot in a forest, a cemetery, or some other kind of burial ground. If that is not possible, perform it in your home temple, but make sure you create a proper atmosphere to invite your ancestors and those you want to summon into your ritual space. An object that once belonged to the person you want to summon should be placed on the altar. If nothing like that is available, perhaps you can use something else, e.g. a handful of graveyard soil from where they are buried, a small stone from their tomb, or a lantern that once burned on their grave. This connection to death and the dead is essential, but you can be creative and work with whatever is available.

The sigil used in this part of the project represents Hecate as the goddess of the crossroads, the mistress of the moon and witchcraft, and the guide to the underworld. The three crescent moons stand for her crossroads, typifying her role as the goddess of lunar mysteries, such as the path of poison, the crone aspect of the Dark Feminine, and her association with the astral plane. The central part of the sigil represents the moon as well, showing that we are also dealing with the sexual current of the Dark Feminine, in which the witch's cauldron is the symbol of the womb of the Lunar Goddess. The torches stand for the sacred fire of Hecate, who appears with torches to guide the deceased through the gates of the underworld. Finally, the key is symbolic of her role as the keeper of inner mysteries. The sigil should be painted in silver and black, but you may also experiment with green and black colors, as these are usually the colors associated with the goddess.

When all is prepared, sit in a comfortable position within the circle of eleven candles and put the sigil in front of you. Anoint it with a few drops of your blood and focus all your attention on it. See how the lines become charged and activated with your life substance, and visualize the sigil glowing and flashing with emerald-green light, sparks of energy flickering all around you. Keep gazing at the sigil until you can easily memorize and visualize its shape. Then, close your eyes and recall the image in your inner mind. Focus your inner sight on the shape of the sigil, see it forming in front of you, in the black space, shining with golden and emerald light. This is the sign that the gate has been opened, and your senses have been adjusted to the current of the goddess. You are now ready to invoke her.

Stand up if you were sitting, raise your dagger and shout the words aloud, in a strong, dynamic way:

Hecate Gonogin, Liftoach Kliffoth!

Face West, point your ritual blade in the same direction, and speak the words:

Through the Western Gate, I call the ancient power of the Dragon, the current of the dying sun, to fill this temple with primordial energies of the Void.
Hecate Nogar, Liftoach Kliffoth!

Face South, pointing your ritual blade:

Through the Southern Gate, I call the fires of Hell so that I may carry the torch of the Dark Queen through the Night.
Hecate Buriol, Liftoach Kliffoth!

Face East, pointing your ritual blade:

Through the Eastern Gate, I call the seething breath of the Dragon so that it may whisper to me the mysteries of the universe.
Hecate Romerac, Liftoach Kliffoth!

Face North, pointing your ritual blade:

Through the Northern Gate, I call the Dragon of the Earth, to purify and empower this ritual space with Draconian flames of the underworld.
Hecate Debam, Liftoach Kliffoth!

Raise your hand (or wand) and speak the words:

May the ritual begin!

UNTU LA LA ULULA UMUNA TOFA LAMA LE LI NA AHR IMA TAHARA ELULA ETFOMA UNUNA ARPETI ULU ULU ULU MARABAN ULULU MAHATA ULU ULU LAMASTANA

Hecate! Goddess of the shades of the dead and those who practice witchcraft when the veil between the worlds is thin! Lady of the Crossroads! Queen of all who dwell in heaven! Queen of all that are pure upon earth! Queen of all the sorcerers of hell! Liminal Goddess! I call you this night!

Come forth to me! Lead me into the dark pits of the underworld to find the wisdom of the ancients. Guide me through your path, black as the night, eternal and never-ending!

HECATE!

Show me the way to the underworld and lead me through the veil that separates the world of the living from the realm of the dead! Light my path through the darkness of the night with your burning torches! Teach me how to navigate through the valley of sorrow, and guide me to those who I want to summon!

Accept my offerings and open the gates to the Other Side so that I may pass unharmed! And assist me on my journey as I cross the threshold of life and death!

I call you through your ancient names:

Chthonia, Crataeis, Enodia, Antaia, Kourotrophos, Artemis of the Crossroads, Propylaia, Propolos, Phosphoros, Soteira, Prytania, Trivia, Klêidouchos, Tricephalus!

Come to me, Hecate!

Ho Drakon Ho Megas!

When you speak the words of the invocation, open yourself to the energy of the goddess flowing through the sigil into the circle. Let her senses override your senses and her power become your power. Sit or lie down in a comfortable position and visualize that you are alone in a dark forest at twilight. You are dressed in a long black robe, and you are walking forward, following a narrow path into the heart of the forest. The landscape around you is foggy, and you can barely see anything in front of you except for the path beneath your feet. You walk straight forward until you reach the point of three crossing roads. You look at the moon above and whisper the name "Hecate." At the same time, the goddess appears before you, assuming shape from the shadows. She is dressed in a long black robe as well. In her hands she holds torches, and a large silver key is attached to her belt. Her eyes are black as the night, and when your gaze meets hers, you can see the Void itself.

She turns around and starts walking forward, and you follow. After a while, you arrive at a burial ground, where the only thing you can see is a lonely tomb. As you approach, the tomb opens up, and the goddess steps into the dark portal leading down into the underworld. Still following her, you start descending a flight of black stairs, which are lit with the pale, unearthly light of her torches. As you descend, you see shadows moving on the walls of the corridor and hear their whispering voice beckoning you to move forward.

Finally, you arrive on top of a hill, looking down on a valley below. You can see hundreds of beings – shadows with no faces and no names. Call out the name or names of those you want to address. You will see that they will approach from among the crowd, assuming the shape that is familiar to you, either from your memories or photographs (or other depictions). Hecate is standing next to you, waiting to take you back to the world of the living whenever you are ready. Now is the moment to tell those who you have summoned what you expect from them. Invite them to partake of the offerings on your altar, and be respectful – they have come to talk to you because they want to, not because they must. Listen to what they have to say. Perhaps they have advice for you. Maybe they will speak to you about secrets and things you do not know. They may also tell you what they need – the afterlife is not always full of joy and bliss. When you receive the answers you sought, or the information necessary to proceed with the working, tell Hecate that you are ready to go back. Say farewell to the spirits and follow the goddess back through the portal. Close it and thank the goddess for her knowledge and guidance. Return to your temple and dispose of the offerings.

Take a while to meditate on what you have seen and how it is relevant to your path. The most important thing about working with Hecate is the ability to analyze and interpret what she has chosen to show you – it always carries a message for you. Still, this message is usually hidden in symbols and allegories. Allow some time for introspection, and, if needed, repeat the working for further insights. If you received any requests from the spirits you have met, do your best to fulfill their wishes – they may show their gratitude in the future by helping you when you need it.

Atavistic Dream: The Great Goddess Rising

Throughout the years, one of the most mysterious atavistic forces emerging from the other side I have explored was Hekate. Her deep mysterious form, her sacred elixirs and transformations bathed my soul with many elements of dark knowledge and veiled power. A lot of hidden wisdom was revealed through each one of the voyages into dense atmospheres of sacred crossroads, where I could experience her enigmatic shape through the shadows. Finally, she crowned me below coiled astral serpents, revealing to me each one of her three masks, the ones of the Black Goddess of infernal wisdom.

Hekate is a threefold masked infernal goddess connected with the feminine energies of man and associated with the process of initiation. She reveals the illumination path the adept must cross to ascend on the astral path of self-deification and inner transcendence. Through this mask, the adept transcends the gateway of the void. This mask also represents many paths to sacred sexuality, which offer the adept a deep communion within the hidden secret sexual currents and initiate a voyage through the infernal tunnels in which the hidden flame of initiation touches the soul and burns it, transforming the living knowledge and experience used by the adept in diverse works of self-transcendence.

Hekate is very skilled in oracular arts and divination. She guides us through the art of dreaming and visions, which help the adept transcend to astral temples and open gateways to connect with diverse elements such as intuition or premonition, and she leads us to proper understanding of the feminine sexual currents and mysteries of life through the process of death and rebirth as an eternal cycle of magical wisdom. Through the oracular path and divination, the adept can handle diverse methods of oracular nature, such as runes, tarot, and scrying, among others. In the deep ocean of wisdom, where the void itself transforms the soul of the adept and embraces it with its infinite darkness in the witch-blood of our primal lineage, the adept can find unimaginable power.

She is the mother lunar witch that offers the path of dream magick, and manifests to the sorcerer through diverse totemic animal atavisms as a decrepit or young woman. All the devotional rituals of sexual nature or dream magick will include the use of blood, but the adept must be mentally prepared to work with blood. Her three torches carry the primal wisdom through darkness to those who dance through the astral tunnels.

The emanations of queen goddess Hekate and the infernal shadows veiled with mysterious, enigmatic shapes always lie latent in deep roots of subconscious realms. My works of years ago in astral temples have provided enough basis to explore the path of the rites of the sacred goddess Hekate, but this time through the second infernal mask that opens to us the infernal gateways to the mysteries of necromantic rites and sabbatical gatherings. This mask awakens in the adept a deep connection with one of the darker masked shadow forms of the goddess, that of the queen of the dead realms and necromantic crossroads, guiding the adept through her shadow paths into necromantic explorations and incantations to the dead.

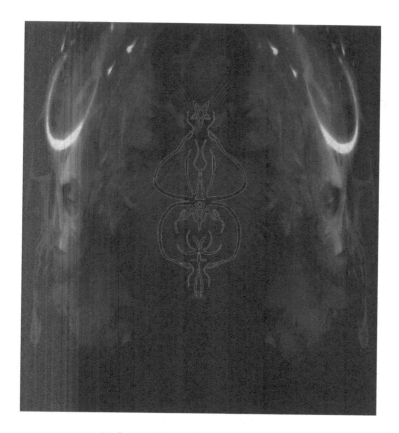

Hekate, The Witch-blood Cult
(A Path of Its Sacred Mysteries)
by Edgar Kerval

Through the mask of the infernal fire, she is the witch mother goddess and queen, who purifies the soul of the adept and introduces him/her into the black arts and cultus sabbati. She is specifically invoked when working deeply with aspects related to astral pathworkings and dreams. She is always looking for blood sacrifice, knowing the potential of such elixir to open secret seals.

When we develop a proper magickal relationship with the infernal masks of Hekate, we transform ourselves into sacred atavisms, and we invoke her spirit through the shadows of the night. We can feel how the triple moon shines and opens the crossroads for a perfect communion, bringing forth primal desires via the subconscious. It's up to the individual to build a great amount of strength and understanding to handle such energies properly.

She is a powerful symbol of the night, magical power, sorcery, and witchcraft. Her essence is the feminine energy and individual focus. Hekate is also considered a goddess of death and blood, and can be invoked with various methods of sexual gnosis and blood magick. The adepts whose magical works involve drinking from Hekate's fountain will recognize the mysteries themselves and discover their paths of power.

The witch-blood connection of Hekate can be described as the core of her sexual and magical energy to focus the essence of her gnosis, which is interlocked in the depth of subconscious, through a proper work. Hekate opens a gateway to the magical current of the adept. The sorcerer dedicating his/her works and magical explorations under the seal of Hekate becomes one within the witch-blood emanations, walking through the caverns of utter darkness.

The witch-blood emanations of the infernal queen Hekate are awakened or obtained through the skills the adept has developed through his/her works via the three faces of the goddess. These works include divination, necromancy, and sacred sexuality, as well as the discovery of the self and the communion with the nature of the black sabbatical queen. The witches' sabbat recognizes that the queen witch Hekate is the primal manifestation of individual power focused on earth. From the drops of her sacred menstruation and kalas emerges the inspiration and intuitive power, which guides those who want to work with the goddess. Once the adept understands each one of her infernal faces, she offers deep gnosis focused on the dreaming state, a very important element in Hekatian workings.

Hekate is represented as the ecstasy of beauty and ugliness of the black night and the black fire, recognized through works in astral temples and sabbatical gatherings of primal nature. She gives the sacred flame of the essence of the great goddess. This flame appears within the adept through each one of the infernal faces in the divine manifestation of power, wisdom, and ecstasy. To work with the infernal faces of Hekate is to understand the hidden mysteries of her nature and her important role for those who want to be crowned by the infernal goddess of the night. The infernal faces of Hekate are of the witches' cult, and the lines of the astral levels of sorcery developed and transmitted from Hekate to men enhance the evolution of humanity.

Hekate, The Sabbatical Queen by Edgar Kerval

Evoking the Masks of the Infernal Goddess

Sigil of the Infernal Goddess

This is to be performed during a crescent moon night. Dress your altar with proper imagery, statues, pictures, and symbols of the infernal goddess to project your mind into a deep state of trance. Listen to some good ritual music and burn three black candles in the form of a triangle, which represent each one of the faces of Hekate. After several minutes of meditation upon the essence of the goddess and her attributes, proceed to raising one of the candles, focus on the sigil of the infernal goddess and visualize it rising from the flame. Then cry:

At the gateways, crossroads of the void
I call you though this seal, witch-blood queen
of sabbatical mysteries, to assist me
in the process of initiation in the temple of your
libations. Oh thou goddess of infernal fire,

Open for me the gates to your sacred mysteries.
Agios Hekate AK- ak hek Hekate
Agios Hekate AK- ak hek Hekate.

Then do the same with the second candle and focus on the sigil of oracular wisdom, visualizing it rising from the flame, and cry:

At the gateways, crossroads of the void
I call you though this seal, witch-blood queen
of sabbatical mysteries, to assist me
in the oracular and divinatory mysteries in the temple of your
libations. Oh thou goddess of oracular wisdom,
Open to me the gates to your sacred mysteries.

Agios Hekate AK- ak hek Hekate
Agios Hekate AK- ak hek Hekate.

Sigil of Oracular Wisdom

Then proceed to get the third candle. Raise it and focus on the sigil of necromantic wisdom, visualizing it rising from the flame. Then cry:

At the gateways, crossroads of the void
I call you though this seal, witch-blood queen
of sabbatical mysteries, to assist me
in the necromantic explorations and dead mysteries in the
temple of your libations.
Oh thou goddess of venomous and deadly wisdom,
Open to me the gates to your sacred mysteries.
Agios Hekate AK- ak hek Hekate
Agios Hekate AK- ak hek Hekate.

Charge with the black flame each one of the three sigils and feel how their emanations manifest within your mind, body, and soul. Then burn each one of the sigils in its respective candle and say:

Agios Hekate AK- ak hek Hekate
Agios Hekate AK- ak hek Hekate
Agios Hekate AK- ak hek Hekate
Agios Hekate AK- ak hek Hekate
Agios Hekate AK- ak hek Hekate
Agios Hekate AK- ak hek Hekate

Now close the ritual chamber.

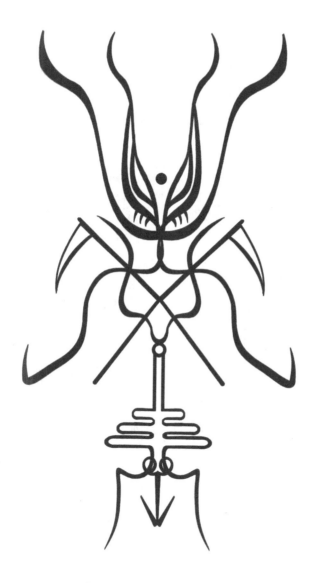

Sigil of Necromantic Wisdom

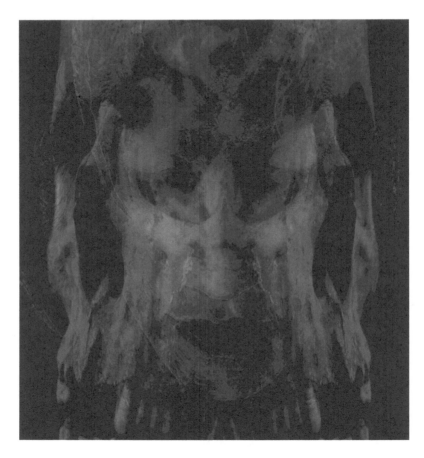

Hekate Trimorphis by Edgar Kerval

An Anubis Hekate Cult

THE ARTIFACT AND BACKGROUND

This piece is inspired by something I found when I was researching and writing *Sat En Anpu*. I came across a piece of information about a green and red jasper coin, the only one of its kind, dating back to the Roman era. Dating back to the second or third centuries EV, it is a double-sided coin with interesting symbolism. On one side is a lion-headed human-shaped figure with a kilt or a loincloth, his head turned left. It is crowned with eight rays on its head. In its right hand, it is holding a branch, and in the left, a wreath. Surrounding the head are two more symbols. On the left is a crescent moon, and on the right is an eight-pointed star. There is an inscription on that side, too, which is in an older form of Greek and translates to: "Michael, the highest, Gabriel, the strongest."

However, on the other side is the truly interesting part. On that side, we have the figure of Hermanubis. He is wearing a loincloth or a kilt. In his right hand, he is holding a flail, and in his left, a wreath. Whether this is a wreath or not is disputed, though it could be a magical tool similar to a chakram. He is facing an image of Hekate. She is three-headed with six arms and wears a gown. She is crowned with modii. Her top hands hold torches, middle hands, daggers, and her lowest hands, whips. On the bottom is ancient Greek again, which roughly translates to "For rapid favor."

AN ANALYSIS

Let's start with the first side, the one with the lion-headed human figure. In the early centuries of the Roman Empire, Mithraism was the religion of choice, the largest religion until Christianity came along. Then, the Romans put their weight into making Christianity the religion of choice of the empire. In the process, they abandoned Mithraism, adopted Christianity, and the rest, they say, is history. Could this figure be Mithras? It matches the time period and historical context, but we cannot assume that. The catch, though, is that there are not that many lion-headed deities known about historically, outside of Egypt. There are a few here and there, but none as prevalent, enduring, and influential as the ones from Egypt. Even if it is not Mithras, it is some lion-headed deity from that area of the world, and given the Greek influence on the rest of the coin, it is possible that it is Greco-Egyptian in some form. This narrows down the list of possibilities substantially. The only thing we can almost be sure of is that it is a male and not a female.

MITHRAISM

I will begin by hitting key highlights of Mithraism for those who may not be familiar with it. You can see a lot of Christian elements in it, as well as Osirian. Sequentially, of course, it came after the Osiris cults, but before Christianity. What that means is that a lot of its traits came from ancient Egypt, and then as Mithraism began to fall, they were transferred to Christianity. But, I get ahead of myself.

Technically it was a Roman mystery school or religion, but as with most things, it came from an earlier time. The god Mithras was Roman, but he was based on earlier Zoroastrian teachings and the god Mithra, who corresponded to the light. In between Zoroastrianism and the Romans, the Greeks had a version of Mithra, too, so it is more likely that the Greek version than the Zoroastrian more influenced the Roman god. But of course, all three tie together when it comes to the development of Mithras.

Let's start with the image of the lion-headed deity on one side of the coin. This is an image commonly found in Mithraism, but it is not considered the most common image. The most common image of Mithras is a man slaughtering a bull. However, the lion-headed image is extensively found related to Mithraism. This begs the question, "Why?" There are several theories out there, ranging from scholars to occultists to students of world religions in general, but there is no definitive answer. The image I am referring to is a standing man with a lion's head. Around his body are wrapped two serpents, which people say usually correspond to Ida and Pingala from the etheric double and the chakra system.

Because they are at rest on the figure, it represents he has mastered his Kundalini, and that implies accomplishment of some kind in a spiritual system, which we will discuss further in this essay. The head of the serpent usually appears on top of the lion's head. On his back are four wings, two on each side of the body. Wings on a humanoid body have long meant ascension of some kind, or at the very least, an advanced human or creature close to human. The mouth of the lion's head is open, and if carved well, it is scary. Many of these images also show him holding a key or two. And that is about it, as far as common traits among those depictions go. Just about every other variant adds or subtracts from this image. Some show him with a caduceus at his side. Others show a globe with a cross carved into it. But the traits I just shared with you are the ones that are the most prevalent. We do have the actual inscriptions on these pieces, though, that do tell us a few things.

The name of that figure is *specifically* referred to as the Latin name of the Zoroastrian god Ahriman. So the altars where several of these images are found tell you his name. We will explore the Ahriman tangent later in this essay. But, there are other thoughts, too. Some say this is the god Chronos. Others say it is not a god outside of Mithraism; instead, it is symbolic of when a Mithraic member reaches the adept level in the Mithraic mysteries. That level is the lion degree. So in that way, it would be the same as the idea of Adam Kadmon or another spiritual idea of the perfected state of being to which we all aspire. Those two theories are both equal in my view. Let's explore both but in a little bit. I want to finish with Mithraism itself first before offering these two possibilities up for your consideration. And remember, this is only one side of the coin! Anyway, now that we have discussed the figure as seen on the coin, and the theories on who it may be, let's look at what Mithraism is all about.

Mithraism was as much a mystery school as it was a religion, as we know religion today. There were seven levels of initiation, and initiates called themselves "syndexioi," which means "united through the handshake." The central image is one of the man-bull interactions, so it seems that it played an essential part in their central mystery. Another central mystery is that he was born from a rock, carrying a torch and a dagger. The birth of Mithras was December 25th, and that date also heralded the new year. In many Mithraic mysteries and images, the interaction between Mithras and Sol, the sun god, is present. Initiates into the mysteries had to swear an oath of secrecy and dedication. They also got tested at the initiation degrees on the information involved in the mysteries, symbolism, and other related topics, much like you would find in a more formalized schooling. Another central concept of the Mithraic mysteries was, quite bluntly, feasts! The seven degrees of initiation corresponded to the seven classical planets in astrology. There wasn't much central dogma, or at least if there was, we have no records of it, so it is hard to say what they believed. Still, the corresponding date of December 25th, the sun, and the emphasis on being initiated into the mysteries were brought forward into Christianity. It should also be pointed out that while they were a rival group of early Christianity, eventually, Christianity persecuted them. When the Roman empire stepped in, they finished Mithraism off and embraced Christianity in the process. Because of this, we don't have much in the way of evidence and facts, but through archaeology and scholasticism, we can safely speculate much about them. The degrees corresponding to the planets show us that it was more like a mystery school than a religion anyway, so it is possible that at least some aspect of it could easily be connected to the Hermanubis Hekate motif on the other side of the coin. You can see how all three, Hermanubis, Mithras, and Hekate, all have to do with the initiatic process and that all can lead and possess secrets of understanding and initiation.

AHRIMAN

Now let's turn our attention to the possibility that the figure is Ahriman from the Zoroastrian faith. After all, the inscriptions tell us that it is who it is. This is interesting because it presents us with two ideas. First, it tells us this could be a case of either-or, meaning the figure is either Mithras or Ahriman. Secondly, it tells us that perhaps Ahriman was involved in the Mithraic mysteries. We don't know how, given the information and material that has survived through the centuries. Let's play devil's advocate, and start with the either-or scenario. This means that we would replace the material above having to do with Mithra, with this information having to do with Ahriman. Of course, there is more information on both readily available. Remember that I am keeping this condensed.

Ahriman is also known as Angra Mainyu and is the destructive spirit or mindset from Zoroastrianism. He exists in the polar opposite of Spenta Mainyu, which is the creative spirit and mentality. By extension, this means that he is the opposing force to Ahura Mazda, the highest god of that faith. In that way, you could call him one of the first devils in the western tradition since so much polarity-based material has come from this system. Thus, Ahriman is the adversarial nature of the person and the mind. This is something that is found quite consistently throughout various sacred texts. So, does this energetic fit with Hermanubis and Hekate, both of who traveled between the worlds, the higher and lower ones? In some ways, yes it does, because all three do have to do in some form or another with adversarial quality (Hermanubis - the Anubis side being bastard born, Hekate - not from Roman times, but not from Greek times either, and accepted in Rome, but grandfathered in, rather than created), so that does make sense from a certain point of view.

But, let's consider the fact that Ahriman was a crucial component in Mithraism. If that is the case, then what function did he serve? We can see one immediately, which is that his presence could somewhat be like Choronzon, where he is the final test of the Initiate to enter the degree of the lion. Or maybe he represented one's adversary that each person had to deal with to transcend continually. Either one of these can be seen as connecting with Choronzon's identification with the dweller on the threshold and the guardian of the abyss. Why that would be on a coin, though, is wide open to speculation. It is only a more modern invention to give mystery school members coins of some form to show their accomplishments in various areas. Before the last seventy-five years or so, the only coins were the ones that had to do with money. This is a guess on my part, so take it with a grain of salt, but it seems that people would have seen the printing of coins to be a luxury reserved for the wealthy and powerful. That's just my guess, though. Using them in this fashion was probably not the first thing someone thought of in their development further into the mysteries. If we look at Ahriman symbolizing this, then we can see a connection with the two figures on the other side, too, because all three would have to do with being at the threshold, a place of crossroads, a point in between worlds - and in this context, one associated with mysteries, and mysteries such as these were common in Hekate and Anubis and Hermes' stories.

And there you have side one of the coin! Ahriman? Mithras? Ahriman alone? Ahriman as part of the Mithraic mysteries? We don't know, so feel free to speculate as much as you want. Written records beyond a few things are mostly absent, so it is wide open to interpretation. With defaced reliefs in Egypt and this, we get a clear sense of how thorough the Christians were when they tried to eliminate previous cultures, though, so we learned from this speculation. Onward to the other side of the coin!

HEKATE AND HERMANUBIS

Hekate needs no introduction. After all, this entire book is about her, so I will skip many details right now to focus on Hermanubis. In short, Hekate was a Greco-Roman goddess associated with the crossroads, magick, travel between the planes, the hearth, light, and a whole bunch of other things. She was adopted by the Greeks from her earlier existence and then, of course, by the Romans after Greece fell. When this coin existed, she had been brought forward from the Greeks and was part of the Roman Empire and westward expansion.

Hermanubis is a different story, though. Hermanubis is a composite deity from the Greek pantheon and is a combination of Hermes and the Egyptian Anubis. Both were soul guides in that they both helped souls traverse the planes. He came into creation when the Romans occupied Egypt. Specifically, during that time, he represented the Egyptian priesthood. Qabalistically and Qliphothically, both correspond to Hod/Samael, which corresponds to Mercury.

You can see how Hekate and Hermanubis are connected and how each one is connected, too. All three have to do with magick and traveling in between the planes. All three have to do with helping a soul travel, getting from where it is to where it needs to go. All three have to do with Greek and Egyptian blending, with a splash of Roman thrown in for flavor. Because of this, you can see why they are on a coin together. This tells us that during that time both were worked in a structured fashion. The critical point to remember is that this "structured fashion" could range anywhere from a structured system like Mithraism all the way to no structure at all, which would be more in line with a religious format in general.

THE LANGUAGE

In addition to the images on each side, there is engraved language, too. In Greek is written two phrases, one on each side, and each one very different than the other. On the side of the coin that features Ahriman/Mithras, the text, roughly translated, says, "Michael the highest, Gabriel the strongest." On the side featuring Hekate and Hermanubis, the text roughly reads, "For rapid favor." When we stop and think about it, the text on the side of Hekate makes sense. Both of these beings can travel through the planes, and rapidly at that! So, putting the images with the text, we see that the image is one hundred percent focused on giving the person the ability to contact both of them to get things done quickly, or at least faster than normal. So, to use a modern example, if you were running late and you needed to get to work on time to keep your job, you could rub that side of the coin, say a prayer to both of them, and be on your way, trusting that they would provide you with fast passage. Fast doesn't mean safe, though...

The text on the other side of the coin looks a little more confusing, and it is this that will occupy a great deal of discussion. First, both Michael and Gabriel come from the Abrahamic system and consider Christianity's adversarial nature toward Mithraism. This combination can seem confusing on the surface. Perhaps this coin is one of the earliest physical references to the blending between Greek, Egyptian, Zoroastrian, Mithraic, and Roman beliefs, which was happening at that time. After all, a common tactic of conquerors and victors, especially historically, is to take all of these things and blend them to say, "See? We support everyone!" Whether or not that is true in practice, though, is another story. But it is quite common for victors to take that stance. That may or may not be the case here. This period in history matches that possibility, but given that Christians would rather destroy something than overtly blend it, it is also true, raising suspicions about things like this. However, this is a perspective we should keep in mind when looking at this particular item. With all of these various religious features represented, we see an exercise in absorption rather than a desecration. This makes the situation even more complex, and given the fact that we don't have access to a lot of non-Christian writings at that, we will most likely never know. We can speculate, though. If we speculate on what we physically see in this coin, we can arrive at some interesting conclusions and quite varied ones. So, get cozy, and let's speculate!

AN ANUBIS/HEKATE CULT

The first thing to consider is that it really wouldn't be an Anubis Hekate cult. Rather, Hermanubis would be involved. With reference to Mithraism, it wouldn't be a cult at all, but rather more like a mystery school, with those three deities as central to it: Mithras (or Ahriman), Hermanubis, and Hekate.

Would the Hermanubis Hekate connection be a subgroup in the more significant Mithraic tradition/mystery school?

Yes, you could make this a cult, but you would first have to decide whether the figure on the obverse is Mithras or Ahriman. Once you have that question answered, though, then it becomes easy. This would mean the cult's central figures would be Hermanubis, Hekate, and whichever one you decided the figure represented. Regardless of that decision, though, you could easily adapt Mithraism's structure to be modeled on these three beings and the lessons they teach us. You could keep the seven grades, each one corresponding to a planet, and do what Aleister Crowley did when saving the OTO: keep the labels but gut and discard the teachings, replacing them with your own.

You could connect multiple teachings with the seven planets, so I see no reason to go into that here. The interesting thing to note is that this would be a mystery school, unlike most, because it would give as much credence to the adversarial nature of things as much as the non-adversarial nature of things. It would also put a healthy emphasis on a goddess, which is largely lacking from almost all mystery schools since ancient Egypt and Greece. The lynchpin would be that the group would have a heavy emphasis on traveling between the planes, so there would be a lot of emphasis on clairvoyance, spirit contact, scrying, invocation work, and related subjects, such as divination.

A heavy emphasis on magick would also be present, considering the connection to that subject that all three figures have. This means that most initiates would be learning some form of ceremonial magick, and given the time of the coin, it would be heavily Hermetically influenced. The exciting part of it that is hard to determine would have to do with the coin's obverse side. Whether you would incorporate it as Mithras or Ahriman, how would it coincide with Hermanubis and Hekate? This is difficult to answer because of the lack of evidence and artifacts from that time. And, following that line of thought, how would you incorporate Michael and Gabriel? They would have to be included, of course, due to their presence on the coin.

Yes, this means we are talking about basing an entire cult or mystery school on this one coin. While that may sound ridiculous, it is no more ridiculous than that we have a coin that shows something like this was occurring on some level, even if everything was restricted to Mithraism. It is because of this coin that we can say and see that Michael, Gabriel, and other elements of the Abrahamic system are NOT always adversarial to other non-Abrahamic subjects, such as ancient Egypt, ancient Greece, Ahriman, and everything else we have been discussing up to this point. That is the truly interesting point, is it not? To consider the fact that before the burning times, the perceived conflict between paganism and Abrahamism wasn't there. There was more effort on blending everything, rather than denigration and erasure. The thought that comes to my mind is something not discussed today: the word "catholic" means universal, and at the time of this coin, that was the main church and only church, with Protestantism a far-cry off into the future. It should always be remembered that Protestantism comes from Catholicism, and there is no denying they share the same root.

If you were to form a mystery school on the information contained on this coin, what would it look like? I realize this may seem like a fantastical idea to engage in when you are sitting around with nothing better to do, but consider the fact that something like that existed! There was a time, and an organization, that worked with all five beings on here (angel Michael, angel Gabriel, Hermanubis, Hekate, and either Mithras or Ahriman), so there is a latent egregore waiting to be engaged. It may not be a powerful egregore, but it is still there and attached to those beings. Speculation aside, this serves as a reminder that what we know and what we think we know should always be considered limited, with our minds open to exploration and not closed off by small and restricted thinking.

Hekate and Mary at Polish Crossroads

Dedicated to Asenath Mason
my first Great Mother
in mundane and astral realms

Hekate: *I am your Mother*
Mary: *I am your Mother*
At the crossroads of your life
Be brave and free
You don`t have to choose
But you can

Why Hekate and Mary in the same essay? From my point of view, you, dear readers, might get surprised. What do they have in common? Hekate is considered to be the Great Mother or Daughter of the ancient gods, or demon in theistic Satanism (e.g. Joy of Satan). Mary is considered to be the mother of Jesus (God or a prophet), so not a goddess, but a woman. I will try to show Her also as a Goddess because She is treated so in Roman Catholicism. We know that Christians have never named Her so, but while watching their masses and listening to their prayers, we can see that She is treated as a real Goddess. Hekate and Mary have a lot in common, especially the crossroads as a place and aspects of our lives.

Let`s start by looking at the Goddess Hekate. We don`t even know what the proper way to write Her name is and how to pronounce it. It gives us a clue that Hekate is a very old being. People commonly think that She started existing in the ancient Greek beliefs; however, this is not true. She is much older than Zeus and other Greek gods and goddesses. She was worshipped many thousand years ago in Asia Minor. That is the reason why Zeus treats Her in a special way. Zeus, the king of Greek gods and goddesses, respects Hekate. He has multiple romances with goddesses and mortal women, but not with Hekate. Zeus has four wives. We know one of them, Hera. However, his first wife was Dione.

In ancient beliefs, we can see that time doesn't exist or that time is not linear. Heracles fights against the giants, but he shouldn't have lived during Gigantomachia. It is time for gods and demi-gods connected with them. The ancient people wondered about such time, and they were right. We can try to understand it nowadays, knowing quantum physics. Why do I write about such a time without time, when Gods and Goddesses existed in many realms at the same time? We should understand that it doesn't matter when the Great Goddess started being worshipped. It doesn't matter if it was in matriarchal or patriarchal times, or if you are your own Goddess (every woman is a Goddess, and every man has his own Anima). It shows that time and place is not important. So old goddesses like Hekate are very hard to understand properly in the Greek patriarchal system. The Goddess is less important than the God in ancient times, e. g. in Greece. Still, in older times, especially in the matriarchal system, Goddess is the first being - not always, because the first Being can also be Chaos, which is not feminine nor masculine. We can compare Hekate to Gaia. Gaia gives birth to Her children, and She doesn't need any male Being as a father.

Hekate is a mother giving birth to Lucifer, and then, in turn, to Belial. It is, however, hard to imagine for people. Let's look once again at Greek beliefs. Zeus gave Hekate special powers - the keys to all realms: air (like heaven), sea, and earth, so also the underworld. She is everywhere, not only in Asia Minor, but also not only in Greece. This is the reason why I write about

Her in Greek beliefs. I want to show that even in a patriarchal system she is everywhere, but it cannot be adequately shown in patriarchal times. She is even in Poland because many people here were chosen by Her.

I called Hekate Great Mother. She was the first Goddess in matriarchal times, and She is a mother because She helps. She takes care of gods and mortal humans. She helped when goddess Demeter was looking for Her daughter Persephone. She helped people at the crossroads of their lives. She is light and dark, so She is everything a Great Mother should be. Hekate can help, but She is also terrifying in the darkness with ghosts, witches, or a black dog. She chooses Her Children, just as She chose me during one of the rituals I made.

That night I "heard" in my mind three words: "You are mine!" (The number 3 is connected to many Goddesses, and not only to Her.) It was one of the most wonderful and hard moments to understand in my life. I was sure that my Great Mother is Lilith (I wrote about it in my essays about Lilith), and suddenly not Lilith, but Hekate said: "You are mine!" During my rituals, I didn't feel love from gods or goddesses. Hekate was the first one who let me feel Her love. I know that She loves me like a mother loves her child. It was such a powerful and amazing moment, and I still feel it in my mundane life and other realms.

Now let's have a closer look at Mary, mother of Jesus. She was - as her worshippers believe - a mortal woman, but a very special one. One of many young Jewish women living more than 2000 years ago, Mary was chosen by JHWH to give birth to his son, so also to Him, because - as Christians say - Father and Son, and Holy Spirit are one being. It's not easy to understand. Fortunately, we know beliefs are not logical. Gods and Goddesses live in other realms, and they can do what They want and exist as They want (not always). Jesus could be the king of the Jews because He belonged to king David's tribe. Reading the Bible, we see that Mary is pregnant because she saw JHWH's messenger and believed that what God and His angel say is always true. She became a mother, but without a human partner. In my opinion, in Polish Roman Catholic churches she is treated like a Goddess. Christians believe she never sinned. She gave birth to God, and later she was taken to Heaven (not in every Christian belief). In Poland, Mary is very important for Christians. She is a virgin, mother, and she is treated and worshipped as Goddess, but no Christian names her so. Why? The answer is easy. Christianity is connected to the patriarchal system, so only the male God is the real God, but what about the Holy Spirit? Who is the Holy Spirit? We know about the feminine aspects of the Holy Spirit. I will not write about goddesses in Jewish beliefs. It is not the topic of my essay, but when we read the Old Testament, we find the mother and female consort of JHWH. We should remember that Jahve is one of Elohim, known as seven divine beings - Gods and Goddesses.

We will never hear about this in Polish Christian churches. But let's come back to Mary. Mary is a mother. She loves her son and all people who trust her. She helps in the crossroads of human lives - the hard moments when we are unsure what to do and what path is the best for our lives. We can pray and ask her for help. She is believed to have helped Polish people in our history during very important battles, e.g. in 1410 or in the seventeenth century. She helps when people pray to her in Częstochowa and other churches, and at literal crossroads.

The crossroads is a place believed to be very dangerous. People committed suicides and died tragically there, so the living need help. Who could help in places where bad ghosts exist? Mother. It doesn't matter what her name is. She is Mother; a human mother who takes care of her children in their time of need. That is why we can see many beautiful chapels being built in such dangerous places. The Mother full of love is there. Great Mother. Hekate or Mary. It depends on the reader's beliefs. People give many offerings there and trust in Mother's help. Great Mother helps in hard moments of our lives. When we feel very bad, when we see no goals in our lives, or we are depressed; In all these moments, we can trust our

Great Mother. We can also trust ourselves because the archetype of Mother is inside us.

I was chosen by Hekate as I wrote this. Other people can say they believe that Mary is their mother. Hekate, Gaia, Isis, Mary, it doesn`t matter, or it matters a lot. It depends on you, dear readers. What is important? The most important is what we believe and whom we trust. Our beliefs and reflections are our Great Mother. Maybe... You can choose the Great Mother, but it is not required. She can choose us, and it is a great honor. You can also choose yourselves as such Mother who helps you. All is your vision, and the truth is, it works in your lives and in any realm.

Hecate and Soul Alchemy

The following ritual is based on the gnosis obtained by working with the Temple of Ascending Flame *Introductory Course* and work done later in personal practice. Using Hecate's guidance to explore the deepest corners of the psyche, assimilating and understanding the darker aspects, those that are repressed and denied, the soul undergoes an alchemical transformation that enhances the journey of self-realization of the Let-Hand-Path practitioner.

In myths and legends, Hecate was the goddess of dark magic. She was also the mistress of witchcraft. Her cult was related to mystical transformation through death and rebirth, and included the symbolism of the cycle of life. She assumed the role of a guide, allowing the exploration of the depths of the psyche through the symbolism of the underworld. In the present work, the energies of Hecate are manifested physically through candles, changes in the temperature of the environment, the sensation of feeling a grim aura, in addition to visions and dreams related to death, cemeteries, tombs, specters, etc., taking the archetype of those aspects suppressed by the human being and allowing for compression and assimilation of the Shadow.

For this series of rituals, you will need: ritual space, a chalice, wine, or some other drink used as a sacrament, a lancet or instrument to draw a few drops of blood, three black candles, and images of Hecate.

Additionally, it is recommended to use a journal to record the experiences gained. The ritual lasts four days (the adept can extend hours if he/she wants to immerse in the madness) and consists of the following structure:

- Day 1) Opening the Doors of the Underworld
- Day 2) Pathworking: Exploring the Deepest Corners of the Psyche.
- Day 3) Dream Work
- Day 4) Immersion in Madness
- Day 5) Dark Alchemy

DAY 1
Opening the Doors of the Underworld

In the center of the altar, place the sigil of Hecate,* the sacrament, and the images. Light the three black candles. Draw Hecate's sigil in front of you with the ritual dagger and visualize it as it shines with a continuous black flame. Use the same procedure to go around in a circle, anticlockwise, and at each cardinal point draw the sigil. Once finished, see the sigil under your feet. It also shines and accompanies others drawn in the air. All begin to envelop you in a fiery black flame which travels through every part of your body, entering through your skin while breathing. As your body gets charged, the energy begins to activate each of your chakras. Once it reaches the third eye, continue with the next part of the ritual. Anoint the sigil with a few drops of blood running through each part of the sigil. While you do this, repeat the following mantra: *Hecate Gonogin, Liftoach Kliffoth.* This mantra is part of the

---

* The sigil to be used in this working is found on page 13.

Temple's materials. Feel the sigil shine with black flames and come to life. Visualize the image in your inner mind as it becomes bigger and bigger, flooding the entire ritual room, becoming a door to the underworld, and in turn, to the darkest and deepest parts of the psyche. Then, before you, envision Hecate as a woman with three faces. She has a moon-shaped crown. In her left hand she holds a torch with a black flame, and in her right she carries a dagger, using it to guide you and reveal the deepest aspects of your psyche. Let yourself be carried away by the experience. Do not force any visions. Once the ritual is completed, thank her and write down the results.

DAY 2
Pathworking: Exploring the Deepest Corners of the Psyche

Repeat the work done the day before. When Hecate is in front of you, she gives you her torch and the dagger. Then the place changes. You are no longer in your room but in a forest in the dark of night. Hecate makes a gesture to follow her. As you walk, you observe shadows of wolves surrounding you and they begin to howl. The sound becomes incessant and you start to get into a trance. The howl ceases, and you find yourself in an ancient cemetery. In the background, there is a mausoleum. Hecate performs a gesture with her left hand so that you enter there, and then she disappears. You follow her into the mausoleum, which is dark, but with the torch you light up the place. In the center there's a stone tomb. You move the tombstone lid and notice that there's another you tied up inside the grave. With the dagger you cut the rope that ties the other you, and they touch your wrist. The whole place disappears, and now you find yourself in a dark place with no light or noise. It is absolute emptiness. Then multiple mirrors appear to project actions, feelings, or appearances of you that you repress and deny, appearing like a movie. Observe them, meditate on the causes, and accept the darkness. Once you've finished, write down the experiences.

DAY 3
Dream Work

During this day, meditate and reflect on the work done on day two. Before sleep, activate Hecate's sigil and place it somewhere near your sleeping place. Then open the doors of the underworld through the pathworking. Once you have finished, blow out the candles and lie on your bed. Bring to your mind the image of the sigil and visions you have just experienced. Keep your attention focused on the desire to continue the vision in sleep. If you wake up at night and if you can fall asleep again, focus again on the sigil and try to keep this vision in your mind while you go back to sleep. Don't worry if your dreams aren't apparently work-related. There's a chance they will reveal some aspect of your path in a different way. Write down the experiences when you wake up.

DAY 4
Immersion in Madness

During this day, you should be alone, isolated from any interactions with the environment around you: family, friends, work, the internet, etc. If it is possible, perform the working somewhere desolate, such as a cemetery, forest, mountain, or beach. You need a sleep deprivation of at least 24 hours, and you can extend it if you wish. In addition, you should avoid the consumption of solid foods, drinking only water, and in the course of the day, recite the mantra of the day. Explore every thought, feeling, or vision obtained through the work of the previous days and try to reverse them to experience the opposite. This disintegrates the thought processes based on reason. After the time has elapsed, finish the operation and write down the experiences.

DAY 5
Dark Alchemy

Repeat the ritual of day 1, and when Hecate is in front of you, she dissolves into a stream of dark energy enveloping you, then disappears, and a dark spot appears in your heart, symbolizing what you have repressed in your psyche. As you breathe, this point grows and fills your soul and body. Until everything gets dark, the energy continues to grow, forming an aura around you. Darkness embraces you, and you realize it was always with you, only you repressed it. Now you understand and accept it. The darkness is you. Once you have finished, write down the experiences.

Guardian of the Underworld

ASENATH MASON

The Gatekeeper of Hell

Cerberus in Greek mythology is the guardian of the gate to the underworld. He is called the "Hound of Hades" and is usually depicted as a monstrous dog with three heads, a serpent for a tail, and multiple snakes protruding from parts of his body. In this lore, his function is to prevent the dead from leaving and to ensure that no mortals will attempt to pass through the gate. From the esoteric perspective, however, his role can be viewed as much more complex, and in this article we will discuss his connection to the underworld and chthonic regions, his primordial features, and his psychopomp aspect, and we will talk about how his powers can be used in rites of self-empowerment.

In Draconian magic, Cerberus can be viewed as one of the primal Draconian entities that can be worked with to gain access to the reservoir of the Serpent Force, the vehicle of the whole Draconian/Ophidian current. His primordial character is shown in mythology not only based on his connection to the chthonic regions but also regarding his origin. In Greek lore, he is the offspring of Typhon and Echidna, Ophidian/Draconian beings born out of primordial chaos. Typhon was the son of Gaia and Tartarus, portrayed as a giant serpent or dragon, and Hesiod describes him as "terrible, outrageous and lawless," a fire-breathing monster with one hundred snake heads on his shoulders. Echidna was depicted in a monstrous shape and as a half-woman half-serpent, and she was believed to be the mother of several monsters. Cerberus seems to be an entity of the same lineage, displaying both the features of primordial chaos (his multiple heads and monstrous appearance) as well as Draconian/Ophidian qualities (serpentine body parts and poisonous spittle). This makes him a valuable ally to the Draconian Initiate.

Greek mythology attributes only the guardian's function to Cerberus, but as the hound of Hades, he has access to the whole land of the dead and can move freely through the particular parts of the underworld. In this role, he can be either a terrifying guardian or a powerful ally to those who set out on a journey to the Other Side. Therefore, we can view him as a psychopomp, a guide of souls. The psychopomp in Greek lore is a deity or spirit that moves freely between worlds and dimensions and can act as an intermediary between man and the denizens of the Other Side. Such deities were, e.g., Hermes and Hecate, and in many parts of the world, this function was also ascribed to certain animals, especially dogs. As faithful companions of man in life, they were also believed to accompany people in the afterlife, often assuming the role of a guide from the world of mortals to the underworld.

European folklore has many stories about ghastly dogs appearing out of nowhere, forecasting death to those who saw them or heralding the arrival of the Devil himself. The Black Dog is the most famous of these mythical creatures, usually depicted as larger than normal dogs and having certain demonic features, like red glowing eyes or fiery breath. They were the Devil's familiars and companions of witches and sorcerers, and sometimes it was thought that witches shape-shifted into dogs to travel to the Sabbat or to haunt their victims. The Black Dog appeared at the crossroads and in desolate places, guarding portals and passages to the Other Side. Sometimes, however, it acted as a friend and guide to those who sought the passage to the underworld – hence the depiction of Cerberus as a demonic dog as well. His three heads represent the point of three crossing roads, which was believed to be a sacred place, a spot where all worlds met and intersected and where gods, demons, and spirits of the dead could be summoned from behind the veil of life and death. For this reason, Cerberus is not only connected with Hades as the lord of the underworld but also with Hecate, the liminal goddess of the crossroads.

As a deity associated with death, witchcraft, and the moon, Hecate was a nocturnal goddess that appeared with her ghastly retinue at the crossroads at night, accompanied by snakes, owls and dogs. She has the role of a psychopomp, just like Cerberus, and the hell hound is her companion in her nocturnal wanderings between day and night, the realm of man and the spirits, the world of the mortals and the land of discarnate souls. Like Cerberus, she is portrayed with three heads, sometimes human, other times bestial, and one of these heads is often that of a black bitch. Black bitches and puppies were commonly sacrificed to her in ancient times as well, and dogs, in general, were believed to be her sacred animals. It is possible that the three-headed image of Cerberus was actually conceived as a result of his connection to her because originally the hell hound was portrayed with one, two, or multiple heads (and even fifty or more). In some of his portrayals, he was not a dog at all but a giant serpent. The three-headed form seems to be derived from the image of the three-headed goddess, confirming the close relationship between these two ancient beings.

There is also another legend that shows the connection between Cerberus and Hecate. According to this story, when Heracles brought Cerberus up from the underworld as one of his famous "labors," the hell hound vomited bile or spewed out a poison-foam which fell upon the earth and gave birth to the plant aconite. Known for its poisonous qualities, aconite (also called wolf's bane) in ancient and medieval lore became attributed to Hecate as the goddess of witchcraft and malefic magic. In the Middle Ages, it was often mentioned as an ingredient of witches' ointments that produced hallucinations and liminal trances. These liminal trances allowed witches and sorcerers to astral travel and induced lucid dreams in which they attended Sabbats, communed with spirits, and journeyed to other worlds and dimensions.

In Renaissance demonology, Cerberus became identified with Naberius, one of the spirits from Johann Weyer's *Pseudomonarchia Daemonum,* and was later included in the Goetia. Naberius is described in these works as a spirit appearing as a three-headed dog or raven. He is a friendly spirit that teaches rhetoric and restores lost dignities and honors. Whether he has a connection to Cerberus or it is only a misinterpretation of the myth, it is worth mentioning because it seems relevant to the working presented here. Naberius teaches the practitioner to live in dignity and provides clear and compelling arguments in dispute or confusion. This clarity is often needed when we find ourselves confused and cannot find comfort or happiness because of strife or trauma. In the working presented below, we will focus on Cerberus/Naberius as an ally in our journey through such a trauma. We will use his powers of both the gatekeeper and the psychopomp to access our personal "underworld" and find the answers to our issues and struggles.

The following ritual invokes Cerberus as a guide through the practitioner's personal "hell." This can mean many things, and each of us has our own "hell" to go through. You can do this working when you find yourself in a difficult or dramatic situation in your day-to-day life, and for some reason, you cannot see a solution to your issues or a way out of what is bothering you at the moment. Cerberus will then act as a force devouring all your attachments, liberating you from emotional bonds to your life issues and helping you see them from a different perspective. At the same time, he will guide you toward a solution or at least an answer to the questions you might have about your situation. However, he will not solve them for you, and it is solely up to you if and how you take advantage of the journey on which he will take you in this working.

For this ritual, you will need the sigil of the gatekeeper and five black candles. If you normally use incense in your work, feel free to burn some in this working as well. The recommended choice is copal, myrrh and rosemary - fragrances associated with the underworld deities, gods of death and funerary rites. The sigil presents the three heads of Cerberus, showing that the gatekeeper's nature is both canine and Ophidian, reflecting his primordial origin and his connection to the underworld. The pentagram in the sigil represents the Initiate on the journey to "hell." Its five points stand for the five senses, both in their physical and psychic aspects. The three daggers typify the three powers of Cerberus to free the Initiate from attachments to the mundane world. The center of the sigil stands for the universe's axis and the pillar of ascent and descent through planes and dimensions. The underworld can only be entered in the spirit form, and the Initiate has to leave all their physical belongings at the gate as a sacrifice to the gatekeeper. This is understood both in the literal and metaphysical sense, involving three levels of separation from the mundane world.

These three levels, represented by the three heads of the gatekeeper, are as follows:

- Separation from the world of the living (sacrifice of your earthly belongings and all things material)
- Separation from the mortal body (sacrifice of your flesh)
- Separation from your mundane identity (sacrifice of what makes you what you are)

In this working, you will have to sacrifice all three attachments to the physical world, although we are not talking here of shedding your mortal body and crossing the veil between life and death. The sacrifice, however, has to be physical, even if only symbolic of what it takes to travel to the underworld. Think about it and choose things that are both personal and meaningful to the gatekeeper, i.e. those that will grant you his assistance in your passage to the underworld. The first sacrifice can be a personal item, something that you value, like a piece of clothing, jewelry, etc. The second sacrifice is of the body so that it can be simply body material, like blood, for instance. The third sacrifice is related to your sense of identity, so, e.g. it can be a habit that you will quit as an offering to the gatekeeper. Feel free to be as creative as you can and make it meaningful and personal. Remember that to enter the underworld you have to leave everything behind, even yourself, otherwise you will not be able to detach yourself from your emotional baggage and find the answers you seek. It is the principle of non-attachment that allows you to see yourself from the perspective of an outside observer and provide an honest assessment of your situation. However, first, you need to purify yourself and get rid of everything that binds you to this situation and blinds you from seeing the solution to your issues.

Prepare your temple in the way you feel is suitable for the working. On the altar, put the sigil of the gatekeeper and place five black candles around it. Light them and burn some incense to cleanse the ritual space. When you feel ready to begin the ritual, invoke the gatekeeper by gazing at his sigil and chanting the following calling:

Cerberus, keeper of the gates to the underworld,
Lead me into hell so that I may face my demons and conquer
my enemies.
Show me the way through the darkness of my being,
And let me emerge reborn and empowered,
Strong in my will and brave in my heart!
I call you by blood and fire,
And in the name of Hecate, queen of the crossroads!
Come to me and open for me the gates of hell!

Anoint the sigil with your blood as you speak these words and present your offerings to the gatekeeper. Say a few personal words when you do that. Cerberus is the hound of Hecate, and you can walk with him alone or invoke the goddess to light your way through the underworld with her torches. If you choose to work with her as well, invoke her into your ritual space by saying the following (or personal) words of calling:

Hecate, lady of the crossroads,
Guardian and protector of the gatekeeper,
Bring your hell hound to guide me through the underworld,
Light my way through the night with your everlasting torches,
And keep me safe on my journey to the Other Side!

When you finish the words of invocation, focus on the presence of Hecate, visualizing yourself standing at the crossroads and facing the goddess. Envision her with torches in her hands and let her guide you to the entrance to the underworld. The gatekeeper usually appears as a phantom bestial creature with three heads or a black hound with eyes like burning embers. Follow them to the gate and enter the Other Side, opening yourself to whatever may await you there, willing to submit yourself to tests and trials of the underworld.

The gatekeeper will guide you through whatever you consider a "hell" at a particular moment. This "hell" can manifest in many ways when you pass the gate of your underworld. You can see it as a place representing your life in a symbolic way, full of objects and rooms to explore. It can also take the form of a person or an entity that will come out to interact with you, e.g. by attacking you and forcing you to defeat it before you can receive your answers. There are many possibilities here. The gatekeeper will not interfere in whatever happens within your personal "hell." Still, he will guide you through the experience to help you see the resources that you already have and make you realize how you can use them to find your way out of your issues. He will show you that instead of waiting for something to happen, you can already resolve your problems by using the means that are available to you at the moment, and the only thing that prevents you from seeing the solution is your attachment to whatever is bothering you. You have to offer these attachments to be devoured by the hell hound to cleanse yourself and give yourself a fresh start and a new perspective.

You also have to leave "hell" with the answers you seek, so take as much time as you need for this meditation.

When the journey is over and you have found the solution to your issues, ask the gatekeeper to guide you out of the underworld. Return to the crossroads, thank Cerberus and Hecate for their assistance and close the ritual with the words:

And so it is done!

The Sigil of the Gatekeeper

INARA CAULDWELL

Hecate, Prometheus and the First Mandrake

Within the Temple of Ascending Flame, Hecate is honored, among other things, as the goddess of witchcraft, the holder of the key to the gates of the underworld, the mistress of herbs and poisons, and the initiator who meets us at the crossroads and guides us as we begin our journey into the Nightside.* This essay, ritual and pathworking focuses on the goddess by using certain of her epithets, names by which she is referred in the *Papyri Graecae Magicae* (PGM). These epithets represent facets of her nature, power and mysteries. Additionally, we will delve into her connection with one of the most famed of the witch's poisonous plants, the mandrake, and some aspects of how this plant can be seen to relate to the Draconian current - in fact; this is where we will begin.

The mandrake is a plant primarily native to the Mediterranean region, although some species range as far east as China. Its type species is *mandragora officinarum*. It is a member of the nightshade family, *Solanaceae*, a group of plants that contains such toxic members as datura and belladonna. Like those two, mandrake contains potent alkaloids, and all three have found use as entheogens from ancient times to today, notably in the topical flying ointments that aid witches in their astral flight to the Sabbat. Mandrake has the added characteristic of

---

* For these and more, see Asenath Mason's *Draconian Ritual Book.*

producing a root resembling a human body, a root that is highly prized in magical workings. The fact that the plant is notoriously difficult to cultivate only enhances its mystique. The name comes to us from the medieval Latin *mandragora*, which became the English *mandrake* around or just after the end of the Middle Ages through folk etymology: *dragora* was popularly assumed to relate to the dragon and was shortened to the form *drake*. While this is not supported by formal linguistics, the association definitely sparks the imagination, and I have found it useful in my workings.

The passage below is from the *Argonautica* of Apollonius of Rhodes, written in the third century BCE, which tells the story of Jason and the Argonauts' voyage to retrieve the Golden Fleece:

> "Medea meanwhile took from the hollow casket a charm which men say is called the charm of Prometheus. If a man should anoint his body therewithal, having first appeased the Maiden, the only-begotten, with sacrifice by night, surely that man could not be wounded by the stroke of bronze nor would he flinch from blazing fire; but for that day he would prove superior both in prowess and in might. It shot up first-born when the ravening eagle on the rugged flanks of Caucasus let drip to the earth the blood-like ichor of tortured Prometheus. And its flower appeared a cubit above ground in color like the Corycian crocus, rising on twin stalks, but in the earth, the root was like newly-cut flesh. The dark juice of it, like the sap of a mountain-oak, she had gathered in a Caspian shell to make the charm withal, when she had first bathed in seven ever-flowing streams and had called seven times on Brimo, nurse of youth, night-wandering Brimo, of the Underworld, queen among the dead, in the gloom of night, clad in dusky garments. And beneath, the dark earth shook and bellowed when the Titanian root was cut; and the son of Iapetus himself groaned, his soul distraught with pain."

(*Argonautica, Book 3, 828*, Apollonius of Rhodes, translated by R. C. Seaton)

Although Hecate is not mentioned by name in this section, she is actually referenced twice: she is "the Maiden, the only-begotten," and then later in the paragraph, she is referred to by the epithet "Brimo," which means "terrifying" or "angry." The plant that rather gruesomely springs up from the ichor dripping from Prometheus' liver is also not named, but from its description, many believe it to be the mandrake. This plant appearing together with Hecate seems apropos, as she is known to be the mistress of poisonous plants. Later, *Argonautica Orphica* mentions that mandrake is one of the plants in her garden. Moreover, the mandrake's taproot digs ever downward, concentrating most of its potency below the surface, which resonates with Hecate's role as a goddess of the underworld. The description of the earth shaking and bellowing when the root is cut also brings to mind legends of the mandrake's death-inducing screams when harvested. These legends have led to stories dating back at least 2,000 years of harvesting the root using dogs, who would then die in the person's stead. Dogs, it should be remembered, are sacred to Hecate, and were often sacrificed to her, so here is another bit of synchronicity. A final link connecting Hecate to this passage is found in the fact that Medea is her student and priestess, and it can be considered probable that the goddess taught her the charm - earlier in the *Argonautica*, Apollonius says of Medea, "There is a maiden, nurtured in the halls of Aeetes, whom the goddess Hecate taught to handle magic herbs with exceeding skill." (*Book 3, 528*)

My interest in working with Hecate and mandrake together began as an outgrowth of my interests before I connected with the Draconian current, which were primarily related to witchcraft. Although I hadn't worked with her extensively previously, Hecate, as a goddess of witchcraft, was one of the Temple's patron deities to whom I most quickly connected. At the same time, I was studying the plant lore of the Poison Path, and I was particularly drawn to the mandrake. I am an animist, believing in and working with plant spirits, and I began to feel the presence of the mandrake's spirit in my practice. I refer to this spirit as *Mandragora*.

One afternoon, I was sitting on my couch thinking about the coming full moon and the ritual I was planning to focus on Hecate. I felt a spirit presence surround me, so I closed my eyes, relaxed, and whispered, "I'm listening." I was given a vision, one of the strongest and clearest I've ever experienced:

It was nighttime, and the full moon was above, with wispy clouds dancing around and in front of it. Its light shone down on a crossroads in a forest, and I could see a large plant in the middle of the intersecting paths. As I watched, it began to move, lifting a head from within the middle of its leaves. The head resembled a reptile's, with sharp teeth, and I knew that this was Mandragora, the spirit of the mandrake. I was also led to know, both by a presence I felt in the moon above and by the plant spirit, that my full moon ritual needed to be a rite for both Hecate and Mandragora, rather than for Hecate alone.

The reptilian features of the plant spirit reinforced the link I already felt between the mandrake and the Draconian current and led me to expand my work on this connection. The pathworking and ritual below draw inspiration from my vision and the ritual I did on that full moon a few days later. The pathworking also draws from the quote from the *Argonautica* above and treats it as an "origin myth" for the mandrake.

As part of the ritual, I chose to dance naked before Hecate and Mandragora. This is a nod to the mandrake cult in Romania, described by Mircea Eliade in his *Zalmoxis: The Vanishing God*. In this cult, which survived into the early 20th century, women and girls danced naked before the plant as part of their rituals. If you do not wish to do this, that is fine. Feel free to use the parts of the rite that resonate with you and adapt the rest to fit your needs and preferences.

Finally, please note that we are working with mandrake from a spiritual and meditative perspective in this ritual and are not incorporating physical use of the plant. Mandrake, as noted above, is toxic. While it is worked with as an entheogen within the Poison Path of witchcraft, there are obviously dangers. Neither the author, the publisher, nor the Temple of Ascending Flame are responsible for any effects should you decide to experiment with this or any other plant.

PREPARATION

Prepare incense suitable for Hecate. Frankincense, myrrh, and storax are very appropriate, and dragon's blood is always good for Draconian rites. Choose music that speaks to you of Hecate, music that evokes images of darkness, the underworld, the tomb, and the spirits of the dead. Decide whether or not you wish to perform the ritual naked. Set up your altar with three red candles (three being a significant number of Hecate, as she is often depicted with three faces), an incense burner, and any statues, objects, or images that you associate with Hecate. Place your ritual blade on the altar in front of you. If you use something else to draw blood, such as a lancet or scalpel, place that on the altar as well.

OPENING

Light the candles and burn some of the incense. Use your ritual blade to draw the symbol of the Trident in the air before you. You may then begin the ritual with an opening of your choice, such as the Draconian Opening from the *Draconian Ritual Book*, or you may simply spend a few moments centering yourself and connecting with the Draconian current. When the time feels right, and you feel the Serpent Force rising within, proceed.

PETITION

Hecate, Goddess of Root Magic,
Mandragora, Most Magical of Roots,
I honor you both this night.
Hecate, Lady of the Crossroads!
Mistress of boundaries and thresholds,
the liminal spaces In-Between;
And Mandragora, Great Spirit!
Poisonous root of the earth that reaches ever downward,
spiraling toward the underworld:
I come to you with offerings of smoke, blood, fire, music, and
dance.
I ask you this night for your aid in finding the Crossroads,
Piercing the veil, flying to the Nightside.

Hecate, in whose garden are many mandrakes,
Who treads on dragon feet that rend the very earth,
Whose attendants are the restless dead* -
Let your torch be my guide to the Crossroads!

Mandragora, who springs forth from Prometheus' torture,
Born of the blood of the Light-Bringer who brought gnosis to
mankind,
Make my spirit light and free, let me feel its fetters fall away,
Nothing now blocking its flight!

Hecate Antaia, Mistress of dreams, who brings nocturnal
visions,
Show me what I need to see this night and evermore!

Mandragora, whisperer of inhuman secrets,
Tell me what I need to hear, this night and evermore!

---

* This line is from the song *Summoning* by Queen of Shadows (Dark Moon Lylyth, https://queenofshadows.band), from the album *Hekate and the Otherworld*, used with permission. This album has provided much inspiration to me.

Hecate, Queen of Serpents!
Daughter of the Ravager and the Starry One!
Hecate Drakaina! In Nomine Draconis, Aid me!

Mandragora, Dragon Root!
Spirit Companion of the Mighty Ones!
Wings of the Witch's Soul! In Nomine Draconis, Aid me!

OFFERING

Add more incense to the coal, then add a drop or two of blood as it burns. If you find it easier, you may add the blood to a bit of your incense before placing it on the coal. Recite these lines as you are doing this. For lines two and three, substitute the ingredients of the incense you have chosen.

Hecate, Mandragora - may this offering
Of willow, and of dragon's blood,
Of storax, frankincense, and myrrh,
Touched with my own blood, my essence,
Be pleasing to you this night.
May it dance before you for your pleasure,
Rising and swaying, dark, fragrant, beautiful,
Carrying with it my petition to you.

TRANCE EXERCISE

Dance before Hecate and Mandragora to the music of your choice. Alternately, if you cannot or do not wish to dance, simply sway rhythmically to the music. Whichever you choose, accompany it by chanting these epithets of Hecate, plus the name Mandragora, until the repetition and the movement carry you into a trance state:

Kleidouchos (Key-Keeper)
Enodia (Lady of the Crossroads)
Drakaina (Dragoness)
Tartarouchos (Ruler of Tartarus)
Deichteira (Teacher)
Antaia (Sender of Nocturnal Visions)
Mandragora

PATHWORKING

You are walking on a narrow, rocky trail, heading into the Caucasus mountains near the Russian border. It is just after dawn, and soon you see the sun's fire rising above the peaks to the east. After a few moments, you hear the piercing cry of an eagle, and at the same time, you see its shadow passing westward. Turning, you follow its path, watching as it soars to a nearby rocky peak overlooking a meadow. It begins to tear at something with its enormous beak, and the ground begins to shake beneath you. It looks as if the very mountain is moving, and then you realize that what you had thought was a rock formation is actually the body of an immense being. As it writhes in pain under the eagle's attack, you see gigantic chains holding it in place on the mountain top, and you realize that this is the Titan Prometheus, who brought fire and wisdom to your ancient ancestors against Zeus' command. You are witnessing his eternal punishment: each day to have his liver eaten by this monstrous eagle, and each night for it to grow back in preparation for the next day's torture. As you watch, ichor begins to drip from Prometheus' wounds, falling onto the meadow below. You see movement where the fluid is hitting the ground and realize that something is growing. As you watch, an enormous plant begins to take shape, with stalks that look like serpent heads weaving in the air so hypnotically that you are not able to look away. You stand there mesmerized, and in what seems like moments, you are shocked to find that a full day has passed. As the sun sets over the western peaks, the eagle launches itself into the air and flies back to the east, and the great Titan before you stills, his ordeal ended for the day.

As twilight advances toward dusk, you feel the atmosphere change. In this liminal time, suspended between day and night, anything seems possible. Suddenly, from the deepening shadows, you see a figure emerge, a woman so tall that her head is nearly at the level of the peak where Prometheus lay. Serpents twine around her head, and she walks on dragon's feet. *"Hecate Drakaina, Hecate Dragoness,"* you hear in your mind, realizing in whose presence you find yourself. As you watch in awe, more epithets sound within your mind, aspects of this primal goddess. A torch appears in one of her hands just at the moment when night begins. *"Dadouchos, Phosphoros,"* you whisper *"Torch-bearer, Light-bringer."* This reminds you that she and Prometheus have certain things in common: both are Titans, and both are light-bringers. You see that her other hand holds a huge sword and that she is flanked by large black dogs. *"Olkitis, Who Draws the Sword," "Kynegetis, Leader of Dogs."* On a cord around her waist is a large key. *"Kleidouchos, Key-bearer."* You can sense spirits of the dead swirling all around her. *"Nerteron Prytanin, Mistress of the Dead."* After gazing at Prometheus' unconscious form for a moment, she approaches the plant that sprang from his suffering. Its stalks are still weaving sinuously, and you notice that they are now synchronized with the motions of the serpents that surround Hecate's head. By the light of the goddess' torch, you see that the place where the plant has taken root is at the crossroads of two trails, the one you are on and another that leads off further into the mountains. *"Enodia,"* you whisper, *"Lady of the Crossroads."*

As you continue to watch, Hecate begins gently digging around the plant's perimeter with her sword. You hear an unearthly sound begin to emanate from the weaving stalks, and the earth begins to tremble beneath your feet. By the time she stops digging, the wailing has become nearly unbearable, and the ground's shaking feels like an extended earthquake. You can see that there is now a trench surrounding the plant, revealing a root that bears a striking resemblance to a human body. Hecate unties the cord from her waist and loops one end of it around the root, securing the other end to the dogs' collars that accompany her. The plant's wailing rises even higher as the dogs take up the slack in the cord, and instinctively, you cover your ears as tightly as you can and quickly move farther back. Hecate gives a signal, and the dogs lunge forward, pulling the root from the soil. The earth jumps one last time in a mighty tremor that combines with a climactic shriek to knock you off your feet. Both die down, leaving the night preternaturally silent and still. Neither Hecate nor the dogs appear to have been affected, but you realize that mortal beings would not have been so fortunate.

At this point, Hecate lifts the plant, holding it tenderly in her arms. After a moment, she looks down at the meadow where you stand. Though her eyes seem as far away as the stars, you can feel her focus on you, and you experience a vision:

The goddess is in a vast garden - her garden - full of more plants than you have ever seen. You are surrounded by plants of healing, plants of cursing, cures, and poisons beyond all imagining. She walks to the very center of this garden and lays the plant on the soil beside her. You see her take the large key she carries, pause for a few seconds, then plunge it into the earth. You feel a gateway opening as the soil parts before the key in her hand, and you sense that the door to the underworld is before you. Hecate picks up the plant, gently kisses the root, and places it into this opening in the ground. As she does this, she names it with a whisper: "Mandragora." You can feel her mighty heart beating in a strong, slow rhythm, and suddenly you sense the mandrake's root begin to pulse, matching the heart of the goddess. Your own heart matches this tempo, and you relish your connection with Hecate and this, the first mandrake. You can still sense the gateway to the underworld, and you can feel the plant's root reaching strongly downward toward it, even as its leaves reach upward and its serpentine stalks begin to sway as they did earlier. In its own way, it is, like Leviathan, uniting that which is above with that which is below. "Dragon Root," you whisper to yourself, realizing that mandrake and its spirit can be powerful allies in contacting Hecate and in penetrating the veil between the worlds.

At this point, the vision fades, and you find yourself back in the meadow in the Caucasus mountains, where the full moon has risen to join the stars in the night sky. Spend a few moments in silence, remaining open to any further images or messages that may come. When the time feels right, whisper your thanks to Hecate, then feel yourself settle back into your mundane consciousness and open your eyes.

Hekate's Rite of Passage into Timelessness

The following is a ritual setting for initiating psycho-spiritual conditions in the individual to open up his or her soul for the transformative presence of this great Goddess. In service to the Great Work, each prospective Adept is inevitably unfolding within his/her self. Every step thereof is marked by intense devotion and dedication to Her mystery, for it's through these qualities that one can move beyond the negative aspect of Nothingness (annihilation) into Pleroma - the fullness of Becoming and self-re-creating every single moment anew. Such re-creation becomes possible in the realm of magic, free from constraints of the linearly structured matrix of objectified existence. So, how do we break those shackles on one's spirit that heavily bind its ability for manifesting its unique vision? By calling on the Supreme Goddess of magic, who alone has the necessary key to open the gates of admittance to Her transcendent mysteries, we shed the chains. Thus, the whole working process becomes a dialogical communication, when instead of having a preconceived, mentally calculated plan for the operation, we choose to open the soul to the stream of synchronicities issued from beyond the manifested world, but yet issuing an unmistakable impact on what's happening in the here and now. Divine traits of

Hekate include both destructive and creative aspects, for she has always been the Deity of Totality, who combines Ferocity with Softness, Overcoming with Becoming, synthesizing polarities of Revolution and Evolution of consciousness, unifying the opposites in such a way that makes the search for the Miraculous reach its ultimate destination and fulfillment.

The destructive obviously has to come first, for "Nothing can be gained without giving something in return." In this case, the Initiate has to be relieved from the false sense of stasis, from complacent satisfaction with superficial appearances, to let abysmal dynamics break through into the pattern of his/her life. Therefore, the Goddess comes into the life of her dedicated magi through the chaotic breaking up of what presumably was solid and unbreakable. These "cracks in the wall" could come about via loss of possessions to which one's attachments are strong, a heavy sense of disappointment in personal relationships, dissatisfaction with long-established beliefs - in short, anything that makes one stop the ongoing psychological routine of the un-awakened soul. In the midst of what one's going through, although shattered, one can gather courage for accepting it as The Way, rather than being traumatized by the immediate impact. If that happens, the first test of initiation can be said to be successfully passed over, with immediate blessing received - greater clarity of vision after the fog of emotional turmoil has been dispersed from one's mental horizon. Therefore, the Intuition becomes the rope leading toward spiritual ascent, and the measure of one's readiness to listen to the voice within and to act accordingly. Thus - as many practitioners of Her nocturnal cult, so many modalities of encounter and routes to self-transformation!

While pathways are many, the ultimate goal is to arrive at the balance between apparently contradictory elements, to find oneself at the crossroads where they have their meeting point. Elements over which Hekate is said to rule are the sea, the land, and the underworld, and so my pathworking to the Goddess is set right there, in an ancient desolate cemetery situated on a hill just above the seashore, as such a place happens to be very close to where I live. But any outdoor location that is infused with contrasting elements is fine as well - in short, anywhere where the space mandala is not homogenous but has got a feel of a crossover between dimensions. An important point is not to be seen or disturbed by people, for this working has to be secretly performed, witnessed by the witch-Goddess and her attendant spirits only. The goal is the complete liberation of the sovereign Spirit, a spark from the Dark Flame, from the shackles of manifest existence, not as a strategy of escaping from the pressures of this world, but to fully engage in its play as a free trans-dimensional entity, who instead of conforming to the dictates of conventional norms is capable to magically re-arrange its rules by skillfully imprinting one's true Will. Having chosen a suitable location, one should first prepare him/her self for entering the timeless realm of Hekate by a breathing exhalation exercise.

Breath exhalation exercises lead the practitioner to experience the absence of air that is awaiting at the bottom of every breath, which is a crossroads between a life-moment just gone and the one that starts anew with another breath.

Fill your lungs to the utmost through the nostrils with air, hold it for a while within, then forcefully blow it out through the mouth in three consecutive acts of exhalation, keeping in mind that with each one you're removing the veils that have been inserted inside the body-mind to cover the true nature of who you are – the unlimited, all-inclusive Nothingness. Perform this breathing cycle intensively for any number of times at a row, until you feel exhausted. Then stop the practice and suspend all mental activity so that only pure consciousness remains. Stay in that state, which feels like a downward spiral into the bottomless vortex of annihilation. Enjoy the long-forgotten taste of non-being, completely relaxed in accepting it as the ultimate source wherefrom the stream of Being is ever unfolding. Then you should proceed with the Invocation of Hekate. Say with strong conviction:

I call upon You who have All Forms
and Many Names,
Whose form no one knows.
You who grow from Obscurity into
Light and leave Light for Darkness.
Come to me in this Night
And lead me through the underworld
Of my souls' dark side!
Ave Hekate! Bombo Ave!

Put your chosen incense, such as black smyrna (or any other blend of your choice prepared for the ritual) over the charcoals in the incense burner to consecrate your ritual space, observing in silence the fumes and feeling their odor permeating the air that you are breathing, empowering your intention to invite Her presence into the temple of your soul.

When you feel ready, prepare the ritual blade and the Hekate Sigil provided on the next page. Light the candle. Anoint the Sigil with your own blood and put a few drops on the ritual blade as well. You may also anoint your Third Eye. With the ritual blade draw the glyph of the Trident in the air, above the Sigil. Feel the energies flowing through, connecting you to the Current of the Dragon. Then start calling on Hekate with the following formula:

Come, infernal, terrestrial, and heavenly Bombo, Goddess of the broad roadways, of the crossroads,
thou who goest to and fro at night, torch in hand, the enemy of the day.
Friend and lover of darkness, thou who doest rejoice when the bitches are howling, and warm blood is spilled,
thou who art walking amid the phantoms and the place of tombs,
thou whose thirst is blood, thou who doest strike chill fear into mortal hearts,
Gorgo, Mormo, Moon of a thousand forms, cast a propitious eye upon our sacrifice.

Then concentrate on the Sigil. Spill a drop of your blood on it, seeing the lines becoming alive, transforming into a downward vortex that irresistibly draws you into its anti-clockwise rotating energy whirling field. Feel that you are being pulled through its central axis point toward the inverse side of the vortex, immersing you in the sphere of timelessness, released of all conditioned identities and modes of perceptions. Let go of all accumulated tensions. Free your perception of their impact by focusing your attention inwardly on your heartbeat. Breathe softly through the abdomen, seeing upon exhalation how the air goes through the whole of your body, merging with the great cosmic space enveloping it.

Then shut your eyes, lower your head down softly, and let it be bent toward your breast. Press your eyelids a bit strongly, to completely shut out any external source of light from entering.

Imagine how you're surrounded by an all-consuming field of darkness, without measure and borderless. It's spread beneath, above and all around you. You're being attracted to it by the force of anti-gravity, falling deeper and deeper into its hidden recesses. You can also feel how it enters you through the pores of your body, imbibing every single cell. You get so dissolved in its vastness that finally you become inseparable from it, mingled altogether with its raw energy. Unfathomable darkness devours your bodily form, and nothing's left anymore but Her. Endlessly swirling dark matter is scattered all around, looking back at itself through the tightly shut lids of your dark eyes - the darkness encapsulated within the "I am," observing the darkness outside of it. While navigating through this domain, you feel both extreme heat, as if burning in hell-fire, and shivering cold, as if in a cryonic suspension chamber, simultaneously piercing the perceiving self, until even the last trace of it is swallowed by the all-pervading dark force, all inherited and conditioned human traits erased completely. Only the primal "here and now" remains, where you forget who you were, how, and where you used to be living in this world. Forget all the whereabouts of your human identity. Realize that you are one with the Eternal Darkness, from the fold of which any given moment of your lifetime sprouts. Having found the center of your being within this timeless conjunction of Past, Present and Future, invigorated by the embrace of darkness, begin now emerging back from the underworld to the mundane reality, through the activated portal of Hekate's Sigil. Notice how fresh-looking everything appears to your awakened senses, just as if it were the first day of creation. Become aware of the physical body as it is, in the natural setting - the wind moving over your skin, the touch of clothes, etc.

Thank Hekate for whatever experiences/insights came to you during the pathworking. Follow with a meditation on Her symbols – contemplating how their significance can be mirrored in the course of your life.

MAGICAL DAGGER

A dagger's function is to cut that which has the nature of oneness into pieces, thus creating a pattern of individualization, Becoming as contrasted to undivided and non-differentiated Whole. The dagger is also used for cutting something grown from its supportive environment, the soil, which again marks a radical departure from the static well-being into the turmoil of potential transformation. Also, it can be used as an instrument for Arte - artificially changing the way things appear to suit the personal outlook of the craftsman - for example, carving the original bulk of wood with images and inscriptions. Look how the same functions apply to the spiritual as well as material sides of life, how they were woven into the patterns of its unfolding till the present moment. Look for areas where the dagger's cut needs to be applied, and seek out those hidden recesses of your soul where its aid is most pertinent, though painful. Turn to the goddess with a firm request to use the power of Her magical dagger, cutting through the thick layers of illusion that are covering the capacity for direct intuitive perception of what is the right step to make when you arrive at the metaphorical crossroads, having to make your life choices. Cut the ropes of attachment to the imaginary benefits of staying within the confines of a comfort zone so that the flow of your life would seek and discover the real benefits that come from spontaneous openness to the ever-shifting dynamics of what's hidden behind those confines.

ROPE

Hekate's rope represents the fate of the individual, being the sum total of all the karmic threads intertwined together, that has both the nature of continuity in terms of its substance, as well as the flexibility of its form. It can be tied in any knot, for instance (and by this it's the opposite to the ruler, whose nature is to be one-pointed, a straight direction). See how you can apply the wisdom to achieve a change in how the rope coils itself in a particular design because then it has the potential of rebirth and renewal within existential continuum. And it's this continuity of self-awareness that connects the triad of infernal, earthly and empyrean domains, and their corresponding strata of consciousness, becoming a rope which one can use to descend to the depths of the underworld and rise above, transformed by what has been encountered along the way.

TORCH

The torch held by the Goddess instructs us that unlike a common source of light shared by all in the day-time reality, the Sun, the journey through the Nightside is illuminated by the torch of one's gnosis. So, one should ponder whether one's spirit is burning brightly and ask the Goddess to ignite the fire of dedication within one's soul. For the nature of the flame is ever to rise up, and the same should be the path of the Initiate - always self-transcending the obstacles appearing on the path with the burning desire for total liberation.

To conclude the ritual, chant aloud these verses:

Greatest Goddess, Ruling Heaven, Reigning over
the Pole of the Stars, Highest, Beautiful-Shining
Goddess, Incorruptible Element, Composite of the All,
All-Illuminating, Bond of the Universe - hear me,
for I invoke You,
Mistress of the Whole World!
Hear me, the Mighty One!

May I be guided by You on this road through the endless
Night!!!

Draconian Sigil of
Hecate

The sigil discussed here is a variation of Hecate's sigil presented on page 13 and used in other workings of this book. The torches, originally included in the symbol, were removed and replaced here by one torch, representing the ascending flame, the fire of illumination, the awakened consciousness of the Initiate on the Path of the Dragon. Another variation from the original version is the portrayal of two serpents coming out of the vulva of the goddess/the Eye of the Dragon, and entwining around the torch, which is also the pillar of ascent and the axis of the world allowing for traveling to worlds above and realms below.

The following meditation was designed for Draconian practitioners in particular, and its purpose is to connect with the Draconian/Ophidian aspect of the goddess as portrayed in the image. It refers to the tantric idea of the chakras, the power zones within the subtle body of man and the ascent of Kundalini, the Serpent Force, through the central channel of Sushumna, up to the third eye, where the Serpent becomes the Dragon, and then up to the star chakra, which is the Eye in the Void. Some of this symbolism is explained here, but if it still seems unclear, please refer to my *Draconian Ritual Book*, where all these terms and concepts are explained in detail.

The only thing you need for this working is the sigil and a tool to draw blood. Everything else is optional. Of course, feel free to use candles, incense, background music, and other things you usually employ in your magical work if you think this will empower the working. None of it is necessary, though. All you need is to find a quiet place to sit down with the sigil and focus on it without being distracted. The sigil should be painted in silver and black colors - the silver image on a black background or black on silver - either of these options should work fine for this meditation. Silver is the color associated with the astral plane and the feminine mysteries of the Lunar Goddess. Black is the color of nothingness, the Void, the fertile soil in which you plant the seeds of will, and the canvas for all manifestation.

When you prepare the sigil, sit down in a comfortable position and put it in front of you or take it into your hands. Place a few drops of your blood on it to activate it as a gateway to the astral realm and the portal through which the current of the goddess will flow into the temple. Then start chanting:

> *Hecate, Serpent Goddess of the Night,*
> *Guide me on the Path of the Dragon!*
> *HO OPHIS HO ARCHAIOS,*
> *HO DRAKON HO MEGAS,*
> *HO EN KAI, HO ON KAI,*
> *HO ZON TOUS AIONAS TON AIONON*
> *META TOU PNEUMATOS SOU.*

The Greek part of the invocation roughly translates to: "The primeval serpent, the great dragon, who was and who is, who lives throughout the eons, and is with your spirit." The chant should be memorized before the working so you can fully focus on the sigil while reciting it. As you chant, see the sigil coming alive and starting to glow with the silver energy of Hecate's astral current. At the same time, focus one by one on the following symbolism, eventually combining it all into one astral gateway. You can chant the mantra throughout the entire meditation or stop at a chosen moment - this is entirely up to you.

At first, concentrate your attention on the central part of the sigil. In its basic form, it shows the full moon, signifying the lunar mysteries of the goddess and her initiatory rites. Inscribed within the moon is the eye of the goddess, which is also her vulva - the entrance to the path of the Dark Feminine. It stands both for the sexual mysteries of the female current of Sitra Ahra and the concept of awakened consciousness and the ability to see beyond the veil separating the mundane from the spiritual. In the Draconian initiatory process, this is also a reference to the Eye of the Dragon that sees beyond all illusions and transcends all boundaries – the expansion of consciousness and the awakening of the psychic senses. This happens when the Kundalini Serpent ascends through the spinal column and activates the third eye, the psychic center within the subtle body of the Draconian Initiate. Meditate on this idea for a while, and when you feel ready, move your attention to the next symbol.

The three crescent moons surrounding the eye can be interpreted as a symbol of the lunar character of Hecate's current. This, however, has a deeper meaning. First of all, the number three has a great significance in the mythology and symbolism of the goddess. Her crossroads are usually depicted as the point of three crossing paths. Metaphorically, it is the meeting point of all three worlds from ancient mythologies – the upper (the celestial world of higher spirits, gods, and divine messengers), the middle (the world of man in which we all live), and the lower (the underworld, the realm of the dead and the land of demons). The number three also refers to Hecate as the triple goddess, which has already been discussed in a different chapter in this book. In modern interpretation, especially in Wicca circles, the number three refers to the Maiden, Mother and Crone – three aspects of the Lunar Goddess. Together, they constitute the archetype of a primordial principle underlying the female cycle and the phases of the moon, known as the "Triple Goddess" or "Triple Moon Goddess." This concept was introduced by Robert Graves and described in detail in his books *The White Goddess* and *The Greek Myths.* In this interpretation, the Maiden stands for the waxing moon and represents youth, birth, creativity, new beginnings, enchantment, and expansion. Her power manifests in action, exploration and discovery, and she can inspire us with new ideas or reveal a new path for us to pursue. The Mother is associated with the full moon and the mysteries of fertility, procreation, sexuality, fulfillment, stability, protection, and guidance. She is associated with adulthood and parenthood and rules over the summertime and the ripening of the crops. The Crone in this paradigm is symbolic of the waning and the dark/new moon, representing wisdom and harvesting, but also death, aging and the end of all existence. She also presides over witchcraft, magic, necromancy, and the journey of the soul to the underworld. Due to her role in rites of passage and transformation, Hecate is either associated with all three aspects of the "Triple Goddess" or with the Crone, and she is believed to be the gateway both to death and to rebirth. Take a while to meditate on this lunar symbolism, opening yourself to whatever messages the Goddess of the Moon will choose to share with you.

When you feel ready, move your focus to the serpents entwined around the torch. In Draconian initiatory magic, they represent the two aspects of the Kundalini Serpent - Ida and Pingala. Ida is the watery, lunar current that flows through the left side of the subtle body, entwining with her fiery, solar counterpart (Pingala) around the spinal column (Sushumna). The left current is feminine and associated with the color blue, the right is masculine and believed to be red. Together, they merge into the golden current flowing through the central channel (nadi) within the body of the Initiate. This energy in the ritual system of the Temple is called "the ascending flame" and is connected both with Lucifer as the force of illumination and Lilith as the passion that powers up the path and acts as the vehicle of ascension and evolution. Take a moment to meditate on these two currents of energy and feel how they rise from the bottom of your spine and begin to ascend upward to your third eye. Feel their opposite nature, entwining in each power zone (chakra) and merging into one powerful stream of force. A recommended way to focus on these two currents is to breathe alternately through your left nostril, while the right is blocked, and then through the right while blocking the left. It is a popular pranayama technique, which helps to focus on the two currents separately and differentiate between them. It is believed that both nadis, Ida and Pingala, end in the nostrils - Ida in the left, Pingala in the right. The central nadi, *Sushumna,* ends at the point between the nostrils where the nasal septum joins the upper lip, and from there, the energy flows upward as one stream of force.

Like in the Caduceus, which is the ancient symbol of Hermes, the messenger of the gods, the serpents are entwined around a shaft, representing the axis mundi - the pillar through which the Initiate can travel between worlds and dimensions. Here, the staff is crowned with a flame, which stands for the fire of illumination and self-deification. It is both the fire of Lucifer and Lilith - the torch that illuminates the way through the darkness of the night and the fiery lust for knowledge and power that is the driving force on the path. In this case, however, it also represents the torch of Hecate - the sacred fire that illuminates the way when the goddess travels between the celestial realm, the earth, and the underworld. It is with her sacred flame that she lights up the way for the Initiate of her mysteries and those who follow her in her journeys to the Other Side. Meditate on this symbol for a while, focusing on the torch in the sigil. At the same time, feel how the ascending flame flows through your spine as a stream of fiery energy, from the bottom of your spine up to your third eye, which opens up to pierce the veil between the physical world and the higher realms. Focus on this feeling for a while, and then move on to the next symbol in the sigil.

This time turn your attention to the key. The key is one of Hecate's most important symbols because it is the tool that is used to open the gates to the underworld. One of her epithets, Kleidouchos, means "key-bearer," showing her role as the opener of the way. We find many references to the goddess as the holder of the keys in the Greek Magical Papyri, and in ancient times, in Lagina, there was a festival called "Kleidos

Agoge," the "procession of the key," honoring Hecate as she who opens the way to mysteries of life and death. The Draconian practitioner can use the key of the goddess to unlock the mysteries of the "underworld." In this sense, the underworld is not a mythical equivalent of hell or paradise, but the subconscious mind of the practitioner, which holds all the power of the individual and the whole initiatory potential of growth and spiritual evolution. That is why Hecate is so important as a guide and initiatrix on the first stages of the path. It is she who meets us at the Crossroads of the Worlds and equips us with the key and the torch - tools essential to begin our journey to the Other Side and to navigate through the darkness of our personal underworld. Take a while to meditate on this concept, and when you feel ready, focus your attention on the eye in the key.

There are two "eyes" in the sigil - the lower, in the central part of the image, and the upper, embedded in the key. In this sense, the lower eye can be seen as the third eye, the center of awakened consciousness, while the upper eye is the higher awareness, the true "Eye in the Void." In the tantric tradition, this refers to two separate concepts as well. The lower eye is the Ajna chakra, the center of psychic faculties associated with the forehead and the pineal gland in the physical body. The Ajna chakra is associated with intuition, clairvoyance, and spiritual awareness in general. It functions as a gateway to other realms, allows for out-of-body experiences, and provides knowledge of the spiritual connection between all things. It is also here that we become aware of the three hidden chakras, which are generally inaccessible to our perception. These chakras, called Golata, Lalata, and Lalana, in the physical body of the Initiate correspond to three points - on the uvula at the back of the throat, above the Ajna chakra, and within the soft upper palate. It is believed that they can only be seen and experienced when the Kundalini Serpent ascends to the third eye. In the sigil, these three hidden chakras are represented by the three crescent moons surrounding the central eye, which corresponds to the third eye. The upper eye, inscribed within Hecate's key, in this interpretation stands for the chakra that exists beyond the physical body, a few centimeters above the crown chakra Sahasrara. It is called the "star chakra" (Sunya or Sunyata) and acts as the gateway to the Void and the bridge between the consciousness of an individual and the infinite. It is the "eye that sees into the Void" and the point of communication between the mind of the Initiate and the higher consciousness. Focus on these two eyes for a while, meditating on the concepts they represent and try to locate all these psychic centers in your subtle body - the third eye in the center of the forehead, the three hidden chakras at the back of the head, and the Eye in the Void above your head.

Take as much time as you need for this meditation. Then look at the sigil as a whole, realizing how all this symbolism acts as a living gateway to the current of the goddess. At this point, you should be feeling the stream of flaming energy flowing through your body, activating your psychic centers and gathering in your third eye before it bursts through the crown chakra in the surge of fiery force. Close your eyes, let it happen, and as you look through the Eye in the Void, envision Hecate crystallizing on the black canvas of your inner mind. Ask her for guidance on the path, or if you have any specific questions, now is the time to communicate with the goddess. Stay open to whatever she chooses to show you. Write it all down in your magical journal, keeping in mind that messages from the goddess usually need further meditation and analysis, and when you feel ready to go back to your normal consciousness, open your eyes and return to where you started. Burn the sigil to release your will to the universe, or keep it in your temple for further communication with the goddess.

Draconian Sigil of Hecate

The Hall of Many Mirrors

Within the dark magician resides an ocean of criminal and animalistic impulses. These primal instincts, carefully concealed from the magician's ego, comprise what is known as the astral body of shadow. When viewed and structured as the Tree of Qliphoth, the magician's shadow is explored in the form of demonic kingdoms and worlds, which can be ventured to in meditation, scrying, dreams, and projection. This same darkness constitutes not only the dark astral body of the magician but also the shadow side of life itself. Consequently, the experience of the shadow is not exclusive to the Draconian Magician but is shared by every human being. The main difference is that the Initiate plunges headlong into the darkness to discover the limitless wellsprings of creative and destructive power within. Therefore, it is the Initiate's task to shake hands with the evil doppelganger, which has, until now, operated almost entirely outside of his awareness. This is what Draconian Magick is all about.

The famous Swiss psychologist Carl Jung said, "Until you make the unconscious conscious, it will direct your life, and you will call it fate." In the realm of Gamaliel, something unique begins to unfold in the magical development of the Initiate. Through the ordeals of the astral plane, psychic empathy becomes integrated into the Initiate's awareness. While empathy opens the doorway to limitless opportunities for seduction and manipulation, it also becomes the key to understanding the many different connections influencing the events of your everyday life. In the Draconian Tradition, this awareness of the interconnectedness of all things is known as the "Spider Consciousness."

The gnosis of Spider Consciousness is most deeply integrated at the level of Satariel on the Tree of Qliphoth. Here the Initiate moves through dark tunnels and pitch-black labyrinths, groping in darkness and wrestling with the mysteries of fate itself. As he explores the Web of Wyrd, he begins to see how all events, places, people, and points in time connect. They influence one another in countless ways to solidify into the events of his everyday life. Without this awareness, mankind has always referred to such uncontrollable events as "fate." At the level of Satariel, the Initiate reflects upon his choices, considers his long-term goals, and takes responsibility for his life. Seeing the bigger picture, he learns to stand in the center of the universe and command the reins of destiny. He has been the architect of his own destruction all along, and he can just as easily become the mastermind pulling the strings of his fortune.

On the astral plane, the Dark Goddess weaves her web through the ever-shifting cycles and phases of the moon. Her sinister rays of Black Light shine through many different emanations, and Hecate is one such emanation. As the Triple Goddess, Hecate is a representation of the three major phases of the moon in traditional witchcraft: waxing, full, and waning. However, these are only metaphors. What they really represent is the feminine current of the Qliphoth: puberty, maturity, and aging; growth, creation, and destruction; initiation, manifestation, and baneful magick; rejuvenation, high energy, and low energy; raising energy, planting an intent, and divining transmissions from the Other Side. The list goes on and on.

The moon and its phases are a metaphor for the subconscious mind. When you dive into the dark side of the astral plane, you are met with a subconscious underworld where you can begin to perceive the normally intangible connections between many different aspects of mundane reality. This plane is also called the Womb of the Lunar Goddess. It is the shadow side of your environment, the unknown thoughtforms, entities, and energetic dynamics that are usually hidden from your conscious mind. This is a great starting point for all forms of astral magick. In *Herbarium Diabolicum*, Edgar Kerval describes one of the emanations of Hecate as the Keeper of Oracular Mysteries. This is one of Hecate's roles as Queen of Witchcraft, initiating the Draconian Magician into her secrets through the dark side of the astral plane.

One night as I was approaching a turning point in my life and my magical practice, I decided to abandon sleep and instead set aside that time to commune with this aspect of Hecate. As I stood before my black altar, bloodied knife, and bloodstained sigil before me, my heart began to race with anticipation. I gazed into the sigil, spoke the words of invocation, and immediately felt Hecate's emerald fire beginning to engulf my body. This process went on for a few minutes until, sitting cross-legged and bathed in the ecstatic flames of the Goddess, I had become the oracle. Visions swept through my mind revealing strange things that I still don't understand: the three forms of Hecate all writing in their books, Hecate waving several of her hands over a crystal ball, Hecate touching my third eye, and forcing my scrying abilities to blossom. My mind was her mind, and for just a moment, I experienced a total dissociation from "Noctulius." I felt a sweet, sublime sense of relief. For a moment, for just a split second, I was free. I was no longer an agitated soul imprisoned within its own constant fixation upon mundane and magical issues. I was, quite simply, Hecate.

As soon as I recovered an awareness of myself, my vision was taken to a long and regal hallway with vaulted ceilings. On the walls of either side hung countless full-length mirrors. Every mirror was perfectly aligned with the mirror on the opposite wall, creating the illusion of gazing endlessly into mirrors within mirrors. At both ends of this hallway stood one grand mirror. Hecate referred to this place rather straightforwardly as the "Hall of Many Mirrors." She went on to impart her gnosis.

> "Your Shadow is a shapeshifter, and you need this many mirrors to see him for who he really is. But that also means he is who he is depending on where you stand within the Hall."

I prodded further, noting the two large mirrors that seemed to serve as the entranceway and exit to the massive hallway.

> "The two mirrors on the ends are so that you can see yourself with clarity, instead of getting lost in many layers of illusion."

The Hall of Many Mirrors is very similar to Hecate's Mirror, upon which are cast the images of your own soul. It is a place for introspection and self-gnosis. The main difference is that Hecate's Mirror reveals parts and aspects of your shadow gradually as you periodically return to gaze into it. Hecate's Hall, however, reveals all of the shadows at once - the outline or "big picture" of how your shadow is operating at any given moment. It shows how different aspects of your shadow may be influencing each other. It unveils patterns, connections, and relationships between the varied parts of your dark side. By walking slowly through the Hall of Many Mirrors, you can see your shadow growing, morphing as it takes on form after form. Your vision is flooded with the awareness of your shadow as an organic process, a living and breathing creature.

For the following working, you will need:

- The printed, drawn, or painted sigil of the Hall of Many Mirrors
- A dagger or other bloodletting tool

- A chalice filled with wine, or some other similar sacrament
- Corresponding incense, such as dragon's blood, etc.
- A single candle of aquatic blue color

Begin by lighting the incense and blue candle. Sit or stand before your sacred space and place a few drops of blood on the sigil. Take a few moments to relax, focusing on the breath, and taking yourself down into the trance. When you are ready, gaze into the sigil. Imagine that it awakens, activated by your blood. It is flashing with fiery emerald light. Visualize how this light slowly begins to reflect on your environment, brighter and brighter, as Hecate's Draconian essence fills the room. At the same time, chant the following words:

Hecate, Queen of Oracles, welcome me into your hall this night!

When your ritual space is charged with Hecate's fiery current, speak the following invocation:

Hecate, Queen of Oracles,
Keeper of prophetic mysteries,
Bestower of visions and insights,
Enter my body and fill me with your Draconian essence!
Guardian of the gateways of dream and sleep,
Goddess of the crossroads between worlds,
Enter my mind and dream with me on the Nightside!
Queen of Shadows,
Ancient one with three faces and forms,
Mother of shamans and shapeshifters,
Enter my soul and possess me with your dark sight!
I offer my body as the temple of your prophetic power,
Witchblood Queen and teacher of oracular mysteries,
Hecate, become one with me!
Hecate, I become one with thee!
Hecate, one in the same are we!

Raise the chalice as a toast to Hecate. Know that through meditation and invocation, the sacrament has been imbued with her fiery energy. Drink now from the chalice and lie down in a comfortable position. With your eyes closed, visualize the gateway sigil as you go into a trance. Travel through the gate in astral projection, or as a scrying exercise, a meditation, or whatever you are capable of. When you return from your journey, be sure to immediately write or record your experience.

The Sigil of the Hall of Many Mirrors

Lycanthropy Rite

The purpose of this working is to invoke Hecate as the goddess of shape-shifting and lycanthropy and explore this mysterious phenomenon through a deeply altered state of consciousness. Before we proceed to the working itself, however, it is necessary to start with definitions. In *Encyclopaedia Britannica,* we find the following definition of lycanthropy: "Lycanthropy, (from Greek lykos, "wolf;" anthropos, "man"), a mental disorder in which the patient believes that he is a wolf or some other nonhuman animal. Undoubtedly stimulated by the once widespread superstition that lycanthropy is a supernatural condition in which men actually assume the physical form of werewolves or other animals, the delusion has been most likely to occur among people who believe in reincarnation and the transmigration of souls." While the analysis of lycanthropy as a mental disorder is included in my book *Sol Tenebrarum: The Occult Study of Melancholy,* here we will take a look at lycanthropy in magic and see if it is still of any use to the modern practitioner. After all, we are dealing with the domain where nothing is true and everything is possible. Let's explore!

In myths and legends, lycanthropy is usually defined as a transformation of a human being into a wolf or werewolf. A practitioner of this art can shape-shift into a wolf form, indeed. Whether this transformation is physical or spiritual is another question. I would say it is both because the shift of consciousness always affects the body, and it is only the matter of how deep we go into this altered state of mind that makes us observe the physical effects to a lesser or greater extent. Stories of people changing into wolves or other animals (theriomorphism) are encountered in countless myths and literature worldwide. People were believed to shape-shift into wolves or anthropomorphic wolf-like creatures (werewolves) either willingly or involuntarily. While the art of willful transformation was associated with black magic and witchcraft, a common person could change into a wolf by being bitten or scratched by a werewolf or through the effect of a curse or magical spell. Witches and sorcerers rubbed their bodies with a magic ointment and recited special incantations, or drank rainwater from the footprint of a wolf. Warriors, who wanted to change into wolves for an upcoming battle, dressed themselves in wolf skins, necklaces made of wolf teeth and claws, or belts made of wolf hide. The transformation occurred at the time of the full moon. A person affected by lycanthropy changed into a wolf or a half-man half-wolf, roamed through the forest or the wilderness hunting for prey, killed whoever they met to eat their flesh and drink their blood, and reversed into the human form at sunrise. The werewolf could be a man or woman, and sometimes also a child, a peasant, as well as a king. Depending on the story, the werewolf was either aware of everything that happened while wearing the wolf's skin or fully driven by the bestial instinct, and it was only after returning to human form that the person regained awareness. There are many beliefs, superstitions and myths involving lycanthropy, and the werewolf belongs to the mythology and folklore of almost every European country. Today we can see the popularity of the legend in books, art and countless movies and television shows.

The question for a modern practitioner is: Can we still explore the legend in a practical way and use it for self-empowerment? If you have an open mind and are willing to experiment, the answer to this is "yes." In modern times, theriomorphism, such as lycanthropy, is practiced to experience a return to primordial, bestial consciousness. It involves practices in which we have to let go of our human nature and let our instincts guide us through the experience. Ideally, we should be aware of what is going on, unlike the victims of involuntary lycanthropy from the werewolf folklore. Otherwise, the transformation will be in vain, and we won't learn anything from it, or worse, we will become victims of our urges released through this work, and we won't be able to control them. Why return to the primordial consciousness? To experience a state of freedom unrestrained by cultural and religious programming, where we are free to create our reality and unbound by moral values and personal inhibitions. This has negative consequences as well, especially if you start implementing this approach in your day-to-day life. Still, magic always involves risk and opens up the doors of unlimited possibilities only for those who are willing to take it. In other words, feel free to experiment, but don't lose yourself in the process.

Hecate is called in this working to help us in these explorations. Why Hecate? We have already described her connection to dogs and wolves and discussed her role as a liminal goddess - the one who stands on the threshold of the worlds. Lycanthropy is also a journey between the worlds - the mundane and the spiritual, the physical and the astral. Transformation occurs within your astral body but is triggered by physical action. This can be anything that induces a deep trance - meditation, drumming or music, repetitive chanting, gazing into a sigil, or using a mind-altering substance. In this working, we will combine several of these techniques. I suggest performing it as dream work. Dreams in a natural way open access to your subconscious mind. If you empower it with the techniques described here, you may experience the transformation in a vivid, tangible way, which will feel as if you really shape-shifted into a beast. Of course, if you prefer to run naked through the forest, feel free to experiment with that, but that is a subject for another article.

Before you start the working, you will need some preparations. First of all, prepare a cauldron, the symbol of Hecate's witchcraft, and fill it with wine mixed with a few her herbs to make a magic potion (this can be water as well). You can use plants associated with her path of poison (aconite, nightshade, belladonna, etc.), or herbs such as myrrh, rosemary, or mugwort. Choose carefully, especially if you feel like experimenting with the poisonous herbs, as you will have to drink the potion during the ritual. Leave it all for a while so that the magical qualities of the herbs permeate the potion. Several hours should be enough, or simply prepare it on the day before the working.

Another thing to prepare is the sigil of the goddess. Feel free to use any of those presented in this book, or create your own if you are artistically talented. You will need some of your blood as well, so prepare a ritual blade, razor, lancet, or something else that can be used for that. Music to assist the ritual can be used, too. Here, it all depends on your personal preferences - you can use binaural sounds to put you into a trance, melodic music associated with Hecate, or dark ambient to create a brooding atmosphere in your ritual space. You are also free to use incense - dragon's blood, musk, or fragrances associated with Hecate, such as rosemary. The candles used in this working should be silver and black.

Finally, you need something to represent a connection to myths and legends of wolves. Ideally, this should be a piece of wolf's skin, skull, bones, or other animal parts. If you have access to such things, I suggest making a necklace or belt involving wolf parts. Otherwise, simply decorate your altar with images of wolves or werewolves, and for yourself, use a wolf mask - my advice is to make it yourself, something in the shape of a wolf, with the sigil of Hecate painted on it. Feel free to be as creative as you want, and don't be afraid to put some effort into the preparations - the more you set your mind on the working, the better results you will have in the ritual itself.

When all is prepared, sit in a comfortable position and put the sigil of Hecate in front of you. Anoint it with your blood and focus all your attention on it. At the same time, start chanting: *"Hecate-Mene, Lady of the Moon, transform me and release my* soul" as a mantra. Send the intent of the working through the sigil. See how it becomes charged and activated with your vital force, and visualize it glowing with the silver astral energy of the goddess. This energy enters the room through the sigil, surrounding you with silver mist that blurs the border between the physical world and the astral plane. Keep chanting until you feel that your awareness has shifted and your senses are open to astral energies. Then blow out the candles and leave only one black candle to burn for the rest of the working.

Begin the invocation with the following words (you can change and personalize them):

Hecate-Mene, Lady of the Moon,
Come to me with the howling of wolves and the hissing of serpents,
I call you to bless this potion and to make me one of the children of the night!
Let your shadows devour and transform me!
And let me rise from the embrace of your sacred fire as a creature of darkness!

Visualize the goddess approaching from the shadows and standing in front of you, accompanied by wolves, serpents, and other creatures of the night.

Goddess of Darkness!
You are the Moon, the Huntress, and the Queen of Beasts!
Antaia! Woe to those for whom you have no mercy!
Your breasts are filled with blood - bitter and sweet,
which flows into the chalice from which I drink
to cross the veil between the world of man and the realm of spirits!

Consecrate the wine in the chalice, visualizing that the goddess' blood drops into it from her naked breasts.

*Let me walk with you through the threshold and explore what
is forbidden.
Guide me through your crossroads onto the Other Side,
where your dark servants - shadows and ghouls - gather for an
unholy feast!*

Visualize that you are surrounded by shades, ghouls, and
specters whose eyes shine in the dark, predatory spirits
waiting to tear you apart. Feel their cold breath on your neck.
Hear their hissing whispers in your ears.

*Mother of witchcraft, shades of dead and creatures of the night!
Your breath is the soothing breeze on the full moon night!
Your embrace is the cold clutch of the grave!
Enodia! Trioditis! Lady of the Crossroads!
I drink your blood from your chalice, offering my own instead!*

Drink the potion from the chalice and offer a few drops of your
own blood - spill it onto the earth or burn it in the fire, letting
it ascend through the gates of the night to higher and lower
planes.

*O friend and companion of night,
Thou who rejoicest in the baying of dogs and spilt blood,
Who wanderest in the midst of shades among the tombs,
Who longest for blood and bringest terror to mortals,
Gorgo, Mormo, thousand-faced moon, look favorably on my
sacrifices!**

At this moment, blow out the last candle, and continue the
working in darkness. Feel how the potion circles through your
body as a stream of fire. The goddess stretches out her hand,
and you take it, crossing the threshold of the worlds with her.
Then, the shades and spirits surrounding her hurl toward you
and start tearing you apart. As your flesh drops out of your

---

* The incantation is derived from H.P. Lovecraft: *The Horror at Red
Hook*

bones piece by piece, you cease to exist, and your spirit is free to rise from your remains and assume a new form.

Now visualize the silver mist rising around you again, blurring the border between the physical world and the astral plane. Above you, envision the full moon - large, silver, casting pale white light. As you gaze at it, you feel lighter and lighter, and eventually, your astral body rises, and everything around you disappears. Visualize at this point that you are transforming into the shape of a wolf, serpent, or another creature from Hecate's retinue. You can imagine yourself as a half-human half-beast, like a werewolf, for instance. See how your hands and feet become strong and grow sharp claws. Your body is covered with fur. Your eyes become sharp like never before, and your sight pierces the darkness of the night easily and naturally. Focus fully on this transformation - envision your whole body changing, and when this is done, focus on how it feels to be a beast. Envision that you are in a dark forest, and your path is marked by human and animal bones. Open yourself to whatever may happen now or travel in your astral body wherever the goddess leads you.

When you are ready to fall asleep, lie down and keep your attention focused on the wish to continue the vision in a dream. If you wake up at night, relax and bring the vision back to your mind, trying to enter the dream scene again while falling back asleep. Write down your dreams in the morning, all of them, even if they may seem unrelated to the work, and keep them in your records - their meaning may be revealed later. Also, keeping a dream journal is itself an important part of the dream practice.

Hekate Ritual: Walk with the Traveler

This ritual is adaptable and can be done anywhere. Yes, there are preferences, but in general, as you will see, it can be done anywhere. The purpose of this ritual is to invoke Hekate before traveling. This is not a ritual to be done just for the sake of doing it. Execute it before you are about to go somewhere. Think of this as a protection ritual more than a communion ritual.

The first thing to do is to pick a location. The ideal spot is in a rural area at a three-way crossroads. However, this is not always possible, so another good spot would be a secluded crossroad of any kind, or at the end of a dead-end road or street. Suppose that is not an option, then in the doorway of your house, with one foot outside of it, and one inside, or merely the doorway of two interior rooms in a larger building.

The timing of this ritual is another matter, too. The ideal time to do it is the night before the new moon, or the night of the new moon. Another alternative is on the waning moon cycle in general (when the moon is moving from full to new), or a full moon. Just about any time would work well except a waxing moon cycle when the moon moves from new to full. This should also be done after dark, but if that is not optional, you can dim the room's lighting to where it simulates night and darkness.

Because this can be done in a lot of different places, the supplies list is relatively short. If you are doing this in your ritual chamber because it is the only option, then you can have everything you want for comfort. But, if you are performing this ritual somewhere rural, late at night, on the dark of the moon, then carrying a lot of things is not a good thing, which is why this list will be short. You will need your ritual dagger, a tool to draw blood, a ritual robe if possible, a candle or torch or flashlight, a pitcher, and a bowl. Anything beyond that is due to your preferences. These are the only necessary supplies to have. However, since she is a patron goddess of the Temple of Ascending Flame, I would strongly encourage you to have the Temple's sigil present as well, to be anointed when you do the anointing in the ritual. You can have incense if you want it, but it is not a pre-requisite. If you choose to use incense or oils, the scents to use would be those of an earthy nature, such as patchouli, or an otherworldly nature, something that exists to invite spirits to you.

Additionally, you will need a few other things. Have pomegranate juice in the pitcher. If this is not possible, any red liquid will do, or simply water. Regardless of what you use, make sure you have blessed and consecrated it for use. This means this is not a last-minute supply to pick up. Consecrate it at least a day before using it. Do it however you want, though, in line with your spiritual tradition. Besides this, have something to serve as an offering. This can be anything you want, including the consecrated sacrament. Finally, make sure you have a key of some kind with you. No, not your house key. A key that you can use for ritual work that is disposable. Make sure it is consecrated, too, before the ritual starts. Yes, you can consecrate the key and the liquid together in one ritual.

Take a trip to your ritual location.

If you are using incense or oils, use them to purify the space before starting. Once this is done, light the torch while speaking the words: *"Hail Hekate, Goddess of the Threshold."* If you can, put the torch down someplace safe, where it won't catch the area on fire. The reason for this is to free up your hands. If you have an alternative solution because putting it down is not an option, that works fine, too. Once the torch is disposed of, pun intended, continue.

Put the bowl on the ground, but still keep hold of the pitcher. While holding it, raise it to the moonless sky above and say: *"Hekate, she who guides all and refuses none, I give you this sacrament. Bless it in thy name."* Visualize it being poured into from above, blackness entering into the liquid, and empowering it. When you feel this is complete, set it down on the ground opposite the torch. Put some of the sacrament from the pitcher into the bowl. When this is done, set the Temple's sigil and the key on the ground in front of you. If you are using a sigil representing Hecate, place it on the ground, too, and take out your blood drawing tool. Drop blood onto the sigil if you are using it, into the sacrament bowl, and onto the key. While doing this, repeat, *"Hekate, primal witchcraft goddess, I call to thee!"*

When this is done, put the bloodletting tool away, and draw your ritual dagger. Turn your attention to the sky above, and confidently state: *"O mistress of magick and witchcraft, I call to you tonight. Guardian of the travelers and guide of the wandering, I invoke you this evening. Walk with me as I take this next significant journey. See what I see, experience what I experience. As I partake of this sacrament, I take you into me, and I give thanks."* When you are done saying that, trace an invoking pentagram of water in the air with your ritual dagger. If you know how to do the inverse invoking pentagram of water, then, by all means, feel free to do that one instead. Draw this in the west, and while you do, visualize it opens a doorway, and when you finish it, she is standing there, on the other side, backlit by blue, but smiling, hand extended toward you. Put your ritual dagger away, and trace an image of Hekate in the air in between the two of you. You see her retrieve her hand, still smiling, as she accepts your gift. Now pick up the bowl with the sacrament in it. Offer it to her, and then drink deeply from it, draining if possible. Refill it from the pitcher. You will be leaving it here after the ritual is done until you return from your journey.

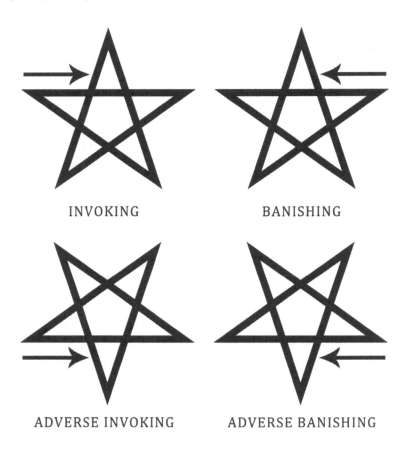

INVOKING   BANISHING

ADVERSE INVOKING   ADVERSE BANISHING

The Pentagrams of Water

Return her smile, and watch her step forward into you, from the center of the pentagram, the portal you created. She becomes one with you, and while you know this will only last until the end of the journey, it is still a fantastic experience to have. During your trip, feel her with you and experience what she has to teach. Listen to what she has to say. Treat her like an invisible traveling companion. When you return from your journey, it is part two of the ritual. When you feel she is in you, pick up everything but the bowl of the liquid sacrament, including the torch. Gaze at her image in the middle of the pentagram, fading into nothingness. Leave, and when it is safe, extinguish the torch. Keep the key with you while you are on your journey to serve as a connection to her.

After you return from your journey, it is time to do a release and closing ritual. Return to the ritual location, but this time, it is unnecessary to have a torch or pitcher with you. Make sure to have everything else, though. When you get to the ritual location, set down the Temple's sigil if you are using it, preferably near the offering bowl. Bloodlet onto both, while saying, *"Hekate, my goddess, I come to thee."* Chant her name until you feel that the energy has been charged with her presence. When that feeling is there, cease chanting, and with your ritual dagger, trace a banishing pentagram of water, or if you know it, the inverse pentagram banishing version. As you do, state, *"Thank you, Hekate, thank you."* Pick up the offering bowl, and if there is anything left in it, offer it back to mother earth. Return home, and when you get there, cleanse the key for use in other rituals, or leave it charged as a link with her. If you decide to leave it charged, though, then factor a regular working into your schedule that has to do with her.

The Cauldron of Resurrection

The Potion in the Cauldron

In this working, we will invoke Hecate as the goddess of witches. In myths and works of literature, witches often summon her name in their spells and rites, like e.g. in Shakespeare's *Macbeth.* In the play, Hecate is the queen of witches invoked by the "weird sisters" who seek assistance in their grim prophesies. The invocation used in this ritual is also derived from *Macbeth* and combined with the traditional custom of preparing Hecate's Supper. Shakespeare often mentions Hecate in his magic-themed plays such as *Macbeth* or *Midsummer Night's Dream*, referring to her as a personification of black magic. This image is rooted in medieval tradition, when Hecate was the goddess of death and the moon, the mistress of the dead, the Wild Hunt, warriors, and presided over nocturnal gatherings of witches and their malevolent spells. The replacement of a modern invocation by an old spell aims to reawaken the old beliefs and create the atmosphere of mystery that was so often associated with Hecate and her nocturnal horde of shadows.

Begin this working by preparing Hecate's Supper - the main ingredients are provided in the article "Hecate - Guide to the Underworld" earlier in this book - but it is also recommended to do some research on your own and prepare the offerings in the best way you can. Leave it all at the crossroads at night or in front of your house. If that is not an option, simply leave them in an isolated place, where they can be eaten by animals, birds, or even maggots. In either case, do not eat them yourself or throw them away like trash - this is a feast for the goddess, and it should not be wasted. Then walk away quickly without looking back. Traditionally, it was believed that one should not look at the offerings once they were served because the very sight of the goddess and her retinue could cause insanity. In the best-case scenario, it was simply bad luck. We will honor this belief here, and once the offerings are left, simply go back to the place of the ritual and perform it without being distracted by other things in the meantime.

For this working, you will need some preparations, so make sure you have all the items needed before you begin. First of all, we will work with the cauldron as the symbol of the Dark Feminine, i.e. as a place of death and transformation. This will be done through poisonous plants and herbs associated with Hecate's lore: aconite, belladonna, hemlock, opium poppy, mandrake, etc. For this, you will need both the cauldron itself and the plants, or at least one of them. If you cannot obtain any of these plants at all, try replacing them with other herbs associated with Hecate, such as mugwort, rosemary, mullein, lavender, or dandelion. Trees associated with the goddess are e.g. hazel, black poplar, cedar, or willow.

Before the ritual, you need to prepare the witches' potion in the cauldron. We have already done this in another ritual included in this book, but this time you will add the herbs during the working itself, so just fill the vessel with wine or water. You need at least three different herbs for this practice. In the original spell, the ingredients are as follows: "entrails of a toad, a slice of swamp snake, a newt's eye, a frog's tongue, fur from a bat, a dog's tongue, the forked tongue of an adder, the stinger of a burrowing worm, a lizard's leg, an owl's wing, the scale of a dragon, a wolf's tooth, a witch's mummified flesh, the gullet and stomach of a ravenous shark, a root of hemlock that was dug up in the dark, a Jew's liver, a goat's bile, some twigs of yew that were broken off during a lunar eclipse, a Turk's nose, a Tartar's lips, the finger of a baby that was strangled as a prostitute gave birth to it in a ditch, and a tiger's entrails." Of course, this does not mean that you should use the same ones, especially that many of them are completely made up by the author and powered up by superstitions prevailing in those times. Feel free to be creative in this practice and invent your own ingredients, but remember that, like in the previous working, you will have to drink the potion when it is ready.

When all is prepared and the offerings are served, return to your temple (unless you can perform the whole working outdoors), light the candles, burn the incense and begin the working. You can start it with meditating for a while on the sigil of the goddess to open the gate to her current and to create a shift in your consciousness, allowing for communication with the Other Side. Like in other Draconian workings, it is recommended to take a moment to raise your inner energy through your favorite Kundalini technique. Incense and background music can be used as well. Feel free to decorate your temple as you wish and how it has worked for you in other Hecate rituals thus far. When you feel ready to proceed, focus on the potion in the cauldron while chanting the following mantra:

Hecate, Queen of Witches, Mistress of the Night,
Guide me through the mysteries of your dark path!

As you chant, feel her energies flowing into your ritual space and manifesting in the temple, awaiting an invitation to enter your consciousness. When you are ready to continue, speak the following spell:

The tawny cat has meowed three times.
And the hedgehog has whined once.
It's time. It's time!

Dance widdershins around the cauldron and throw in the first herb saying:

To you, Hecate, I offer this sacrament,
Here is ... (the name of the plant) ... in your honor,
Bless it with your power and make my potion strong!

As you stir the potion, chant the following:

Double, double toil and trouble,
Fire burn, and cauldron bubble.

When this is done, add the second herb to the potion,
repeating the whole procedure:

To you, Hecate, I offer this sacrament,
Here is ... (the name of the plant) ... in your honor,
Bless it with your power and make my potion strong!

As you stir the potion, chant the following:

Double, double toil and trouble,
Fire burn, and cauldron bubble.

And then add the third herb, performing the same action:

To you, Hecate, I offer this sacrament,
Here is ... (the name of the plant) ... in your honor,
Bless it with your power and make my potion strong!

As you stir the potion, chant the following:

Double, double toil and trouble,
Fire burn, and cauldron bubble.

Finally, add a few drops of your blood, saying:

I charge this potion by the Blood of the Dragon,
And in the name of the Dragon!
The charm is finished.

While you do all that, visualize silver mist entering the temple through the cauldron and surrounding you, blurring the border between the mundane and the astral. With the addition of each herb, the mist becomes thicker and more tangible. When you finish the spell, close your eyes and envision the goddess taking shape in front of you from this astral mist. You can envision her in her traditional form, i.e. as three women or one woman with three animal heads, or you can visualize her as a witch dressed in a long black hooded robe, with her face hidden under the hood. Envision that she blesses the sacrament on the altar and then drink it, visualizing that you are drinking her potion that brings death and liberation from the bonds of the flesh.

Lie down now if you want to, or continue the working in a meditative posture, and focus on your third eye. Feel how it opens, the whole world around you disappears, and you find yourself standing at the point of three crossing roads, facing Hecate, who is standing next to her cauldron. It is the same cauldron as the one on your altar, but here it is bigger, large enough to boil a human being. And this is exactly what happens - Hecate shows you to get into the cauldron, which is still filled with her potion, and sets her fire under it. This process of boiling the Initiate in the cauldron has a long tradition in various rites of passage. It is mentioned e.g. in shamanic mysteries of dismemberment and resurrection, and in Celtic myths of Cerridwen, whose cauldron contains the mystery of transformation and rebirth (in one of myths, it has the power to resurrect the corpses of dead warriors placed in it). The cauldron of Hecate is symbolic of the womb of the Dark Mother, the place of death and decomposition, but also transformation and resurrection, containing the mystery of the eternal cycle of nature. Having all that in mind, visualize that you immerse yourself in her potion as you enter the cauldron, letting yourself be killed, transformed, and then resurrected. Feel the heat burning your body and your flesh dropping off of it piece by piece as you remain in a dark, warm place, which feels like a woman's womb. Continue this visualization until there is nothing left and you are free from the bonds of the flesh.

Then rise and join the goddess and her spectral retinue in their nocturnal passage through the night. Let her guide you through the experience and initiate you in her mysteries of the craft. Visualize that while walking with her, your body crystallizes anew with each step, becoming more real, more tangible, and stronger than ever before. All the weaknesses, diseases, imperfections, and all that does not serve you in your mundane life you have been dissolved in the cauldron. Now you are free to shape and mold yourself as you wish. Let Hecate guide you through this process and open yourself to whatever she chooses to show you. Write down your visions and insights after the working, or do it while staying in the charged, meditative state of mind. When you feel ready to finish the ritual, close it with the words:

And so it is done!

The potion in the cauldron should be drunk or offered to the earth. Like in the case of other offerings, it should not be poured away and wasted.

Draconian Hecate

Temple of Ascending Flame Contributors

Asenath Mason is a writer and artist. Author of many books and essays on esoteric, religious and mythological subjects, with a particular focus on the Left Hand Path philosophy, Luciferian Spirituality and Draconian Tradition. Active practitioner of Occult Arts and teacher offering personal consultations and initiations into the Draconian Current. Founder and coordinator of the Temple of Ascending Flame, a platform for individuals around the world who want to share certain aspects of their work within Draconian Tradition with other adepts on the path and for those who need guidance into Draconian initiatory magic. Co-author and editor of a number of anthologies and occult magazines. Co-owner of the publishing house Draco Press (with Bill Duvendack). She is also a varied artist, working with digital media, and themes of her artwork include various gothic, fantasy and esoteric concepts. Contact & more information:
www.asenathmason.com

Roberto Ruiz Blum, a 23-year-old Ecuadorian, is an economics student and student activist. He is a practitioner of the Left Hand Path and a member of the Temple of Ascending Flame. Since his adolescence, he studied various subjects such as Qabbalah, astrology, tarot, Kundalini yoga, Taoism and various meditation practices. He was a member of the Rosacruz AMORC Order and is now a Freemason. Contact: **rober.689@hotmail.es**

Bill Duvendack is an internationally known astrologer, editor, psychic, presenter, publisher, teacher, and author. He has presented in many venues, ranging from colleges and high schools to national and international conferences. He is the author of over a dozen published books on modern spirituality, with more soon to be released. He has had over four dozen essays published in various anthologies, and his magical writings have been translated into 6 languages, with more coming out soon. He regularly teaches digital courses on magick, astrology, and modern spirituality. He has been interviewed by the NY Times, RTE 1, and has made many TV and radio appearances. For more information about him, please consult his website: **www.418ascendant.com**

Inara Cauldwell is a writer, occultist, and musician living in Seattle. Her artistic pursuits are strongly influenced by her magical life and practice, as well as by her eclectic background as a student of philosophy, the Arabic language, and Mesopotamian mythology. She is a member of the Toronto-based artist collective ARTUS, contributing as a researcher and as a writer of horror, erotica and occultism.
Email: **inara.cauldwell@gmail.com**
Website: **artuscollective.org/inara-cauldwell**

Denerah Erzebet is the author of *Rites of Astaroth* and *VOVIN: Reflections on the Temple of Ascending Flame*, both published by Draco Press. Erzebet specializes in contemporary manifestations of the Typhonian Tradition, including connections to Goetia, Enochian magic and sexual sorcery.
Contact Information: **jordano.bortolotto@gmail.com**

Keona Kai'Nathera is a HPS in the BOS, a member of the Temple of Ascending Flame. She has over 30 years in the occult. Her work is focused on Necromancy, Blood Magick, Divination and she is a budding herbalist. You can find her on YT under **Serenity Keona** or on IG at **keonakainathera.**

Noctulius Isaac is a 23-year-old writer, Draconian magician, cancer survivor, and black metal musician living in Chicago.

His spiritual path began with Charismatic Christianity and shifted over the years into practices of Theistic Satanism and black magick. The majority of his magick is focused on the work of Temple of Ascending Flame, as well as releasing his first black metal album.

stylzeisawesome@gmail.com
instagram.com/dripstylze666

Edgar Kerval is an author and musician coming from Colombia, South America. He has been working through more than 20 years with diverse paths of sorcery. He focuses on elements regarding saturnian gnosis dealing with death entities from diverse pantheons. Also, he works on many ritual ambient musical projects such as EMME YA, THE RED PATH, ARCHAIC:, among others. He has his own small publishing house called SIRIUS LIMITED ESOTERICA, in which he publishes some of his works and the books of other well-known authors. He has participated in II and III International Left Hand Path Consortium in Atlanta and St Louis respectively. He has released more than 9 books and participated in several anthologies.

www.emmeya111.bandcamp.com
siriuslimitedesoterica.blogspot.com

Mike Musoke, 31, is a professional Food Scientist and an expert in Child Malnutrition. He has worked with different NGOs in Malawi and Uganda to assist rural communities cope with distressing effects of Malnutrition among children. He has been a student and practitioner of various Pagan cultures for 5 years and Draconian magic for close to two years now. He is a devotee of the Goddess Hecate and walks with Belphegor, Azazel and Lucifer. He has a very active relationship with the infernal lords and credits all blessings accomplishments in his life to them. As a Priest of the Temple of Ascending Flame and the interim coordinator of the Draconian sorority in Malawi, Mike hopes to open an esoteric wellness and education centre in the future. Inquiries may be directed to:

mkmusoke@gmail.com

Satoriel Abraxas is an initiate of the Temple of Ascending Flame. His work involves exploring the realms of Gnostic spirituality & esoteric praxis, both past and present. Lucifer's friend and a devotee of chthonic Deities (such as Hecate). Ceremonial magician & student of Qliphothic Cabala. He enjoys outdoor workings in power spots and silent retreats deep in nature. He believes that magical energy is best channelled into art, and tries to become a vehicle for its expression in his own creative actions.
For any contact/information check:
facebook.com/satoriel.abraxas.1

Selene-Lilith vel Belayla Rakoczy (Barbara Selene Występek) was born in 1970 in Poland; she is a teacher of Polish language and a poet; a priestess of the Temple of Ascending Flame since 2012, initiated by Asenath Mason in 2013; a member of House Rakoczy; interested in psychology, antique history, Jungian philosophy, beliefs of many nations, reading Tarot, runes and playing her favourite 200-years old grand piano; necromancer, connected to LHP magick.

SPECIAL CONTRIBUTION

Jack Grayle is a working sorcerer who teaches courses on the magic of Hekate and the PGM at:
www.theblackthorneschool.com

He is the author of the grimoire *The Hekataeon*, and his writings have been published by Ixaxaar, Aeon Sophia, Hadean Press, Anathema, and Sabbatica. He has been invited to present at numerous events such as Black Flame PDX, the International Left Hand Path Consortium, and the Welsh Occult Conference. Updates on his work may be found at **www.jackgrayle.com**

Hekate the Adversary

"Moloch, sceptered king,
Stood up, the strongest and the fiercest spirit
That fought in heav'n; now fiercer by despair;
His trust was with the eternal to be deemed
Equal in strength; and rather than be less
Cared not to be at all; with that care lost
Went all his fear: of god, or hell, or worst
He reck'd not, and these words, thereafter spake:
'My sentence is for open war.'"

(*Paradise Lost*, Book II: 43-51, John Milton)

John Milton was blind when he dictated the passage above in 1667. He said his goal in writing *Paradise Lost* and *Paradise Regained* was "to justify the ways of God to man." To that end, he declaimed ten thousand lines to his daughter, who transcribed them all into what became his masterwork. This epic recital stands as one of the monumental feats in world literature, rivaled only by Homer's *Iliad* and *Odyssey*, which were allegedly recited by the blind bard nearly three thousand years ago.

And yet, for all its virtues, Milton's epic poem is not perfect, having a well-recognized flaw, which is this: His fallen angels steal the show. While he portrayed Michael, Gabriel, and the rest with great skill, ironically, Milton's arrogant Lucifer, brooding Belial, and bellicose Moloch impress the reader much more than their virtuous counterparts.

Take Christ's promise to his heavenly father:

> "But whom thou hatest, I hate, and can put on
> Thy terrors, as I put thy mildness on,
> Image of thee in all things, and shall soon,
> Armed with thy might, rid Heaven of these rebell'd,
> To their prepared ill mansion driven down
> To chains of Darkness, and the undying Worm[.]"*

The verse scans. The sentiment is stirring. But how can it compare to Moloch's snarl?

My sentence is for open war.

There is something in that line that makes the blood sing. And more than that: it makes the heart beat faster in sympathy to the antagonist's wrathful cry. Why should that be? Why should the heart respond to defiance more than to obedience? And yet it does. Such verse does more than entertain and enlighten; it enflames the reader's spirit.

Very few fiction characters can ignite the reader with such fierce sympathy – and even fewer characters in real life. When they do, they are almost always loners, outnumbered and outgunned; outsiders who speak with open contempt to those with authority over them. The context is almost always adversarial.

The heroes (or rather, anti-heroes) of yesteryear live on in our memories. And presumably, the (anti-) heroes of our age will, over time, become known and appreciated as well, as will the bloody banners they fought under The Red Star. The Crescent Moon. The Black Dragon.

---

* Milton, John, *Paradise Lost*, Book 4, line 734-9 (Signet Classics, 2010), p. 154.

DRAGON LADY

When I first met Asenath Mason, she was not what I expected. I was attending the International Left Hand Path Consortium in St. Louis in 2017, browsing through vendor stalls outside the notorious Lemp Mansion, a hulking edifice with a hundred-year history of orgies and suicides that earned it a reputation as one of the most haunted houses in America.

Asenath had a reputation, too. She is the author of the popular *Liber Thagirion*, *Grimoire of Tiamat*, and *Rites of Lucifer*, among other works of Draconian spirituality. In addition, her artwork sets her apart, in a field primarily dominated by men, as a talented creatrix of terrifying and sensual images whose unique expression of infernal immanence rivals those of Hieronymous Bosch.

I'm not sure what I was expecting – perhaps someone in velvet robes with heavily Kohled eyes – but it wasn't what I got. Asenath was slim and lovely, dressed in a silver sheath dress. She moved with an elegant economy; her eyes were bright and watchful. When she spoke, her voice had a low thrum, like an idling Ferrari.

I introduced myself clumsily, and she graciously let me join her at her table. I plied her with questions, and she answered them good-naturedly. She talked about her decision to start the Temple of Ascending Flame and how she had grown it over the years. She described her dedication to those spirits - Lucifer, Lilith, Leviathan - that are traditionally decried as embodiments of evil, but who in her system embody gnosis of the mind and elevation of the soul, and above all else, liberation from constraints - spiritual or otherwise.

Sitting there in her presence, it would be easy to assume that the soft-spoken woman in the silver dress was, at heart, similar to the rest of us who muddle along, doing the best we can with what we're given, and trying to make nice with the powers that be. Her grace and easy charm would support that assumption, which many people might make.

But those people would be wrong. They would be wrong because they would be ignoring one single fact that sets her - and those like her - apart from almost everyone else in the West:

Asenath's voice - like Moloch's - is for open war.

Asenath's art, writing, and rituals reflect her spirituality, and her spirituality is predicated upon an adversarial principle. And she is not alone.

Many would claim that there are hundreds of spiritual traditions in the West, but in fact, there are really only two: Those which support the ruling paradigm and those which reject it. In the twentieth century, the population of the second group was a sliver of the first. In the twenty-first century, that ratio may well reverse.

With every day that passes, we have less privacy than we had before, less political agency, less opportunity for independent action. The powers that infringe on our rights are legion but primarily consist of corporate and national interests whose invasive reach extends deeper into our lives than at any time within recent memory. All of us know this, but few of us choose lifestyles which actively oppose the endless encroachment of these implacable powers. Those who do so politically are deemed outsiders, anarchists, and dissidents. Those who do so spiritually are deemed adversarialists.

The notes that follow suggest two things: first, that there exists in our Western culture a legitimate adversarialist spiritual tradition, and second, that the goddess Hekate has been - and can be again - a fixture of that tradition, and one whose presence can provide access to a current of untapped personal power and potential to rebel against (and even reverse) our fates.

ADVERSARIALISM

What is an adversarialist spirituality? I suggest that it is one whose defining characteristic is that it opposes the central tenets of the predominant spiritual paradigm of the time. In other words, *it must explicitly reject* - and not merely amend or ignore - the dominant tradition.

Thus, for example, the rise of the Cult of the Emperor in ancient Rome was *not* adversarialist: though the concept of deifying political leaders was new to post-Republic Roman citizens. In some ways, it was simply an extreme form of ancestor worship which has always been common in Latin funeral traditions since time immemorial. More importantly, it ultimately did not contradict the existing state cult of the twelve Olympians; it only expanded it to include an ever-growing pantheon of divine rulers (along with the emperors' now-divine parents, children, wives, and lovers).*

By contrast, Zoroastrianism was partially adversarialist since it upended both the existing pantheon of Persian gods and the tradition of animal sacrifice that supported it. Zoroaster provided a new overgod (*Ahura Mazda*) and divided existing deities into good *ahuras* and bad *daevas*, allowing worship to be given to the former but denied to the latter, which were rejected as bringers of chaos and disorder.

And, of course, Christianity was adversarialist too in its infancy. It was not entirely new, of course: it blended apocryphal Judaism with redemptive elements of the pagan mystery tradition, the abstraction of Neoplatonism, and the uncompromising morality of the Persian fire cult; yet its central tenet was an unqualified rejection of the entire schema of paganism. Christianity remained adversarialist until declared to be the official religion of the Roman Empire by

---

* Hadrian's surprisingly successful deification of Antinous is a good example of divine status being granted to a lover.

Theodosius I in 393 AD, at which point the fox became the hound, and Christian emperors enthusiastically began to snuff out all vestiges of the pagan state cults, succeeding finally with the closure of the Temple of Isis in Philae, Egypt, in 536 AD.

However, it is important to note that even when these pagan cults were being eradicated, they themselves were never adversarialist against the now-dominant Christian regime. The pagan paradigm was inclusive and syncretic: the worship of new gods did not refute the validity of worshipping old ones. And when such worship was banned, the reasons were purely political: i.e. Roman citizens were banned from participating in foreign cults until late antiquity, but this ban was not because the Eastern and Roman cults were incompatible, but because the praxis of the Eastern cults was considered by the Roman senate to be distasteful and dangerous, and was therefore barred to both preserve the Roman identity and protect its citizens from the perceived excesses of the Eastern ecstatic traditions.

And yet, Roman and Eastern pagan traditions themselves were not antithetical. When eventually the ban on foreign worship was lifted by a series of erratic and short-lived emperors, the worshippers of Serapis, Kybelle, and Elagabal co-existed peacefully (though briefly) alongside those of Jupiter, Juno, and Venus in Rome. Indeed, their devotees were often one and the same.

Did an adversarialist tradition exist in the West after Theodosius? I believe so and submit four instances. The first would be certain Gnostic traditions developed as heretical outgrowths of Judaism and Christianity in the millennium following late antiquity.

Here it should be pointed out that heresies should not universally be considered adversarial unless they intentionally reject the primary tenets of the predominant paradigm. For example, Christian Arianism would *not* have been an adversarial heresy because its concept of Christ as distinct from and subordinate to God the Father refutes Trinitarianism, but not the core doctrine of Christianity itself (i.e. that humanity is redeemed by Christ's death on the cross).

By the same token, Ophite Gnosticism *would* have been an adversarial tradition. The Ophites held that the true Trinity was not God the Father, Son, and the Holy Spirit, but an ungraspable source of sacred light, the feminine creatrix who ejected all material into the cosmos, and a deformed and evil demiurge who ignorantly fashioned mortals into unclean cages of flesh and bone, from which they can escape only by perfecting their knowledge of their true origin. This belief entirely refutes both orthodox Christianity and Judaism on every point. It is inherently antagonistic toward its parent; they cannot co-exist.

Likewise, Catharism was adversarial: its central doctrine was that there were two gods, the good Christ and the Satanic YHVH. This undercut the foundational dogma of both Byzantine and Roman Catholic Christianity, and the established Church spent the better part of the Medieval age violently purging Catharism by fire and sword from Western Europe in general and Southern France in particular. In some regions, fully one-fourth of the population was exterminated in the name of doctrinal purity.

Other examples exist. From its inception in the seventh century, Islam - although recognizing the figures of God, Christ, and Mary - nevertheless was entirely adversarial to Jewish, Christian, and Persian regimes and remained so until it replaced them in the Near East.

For the same reasons, the rationalist atheism forcefully articulated by Nietzsche in *Thus Spake Zarathustra* constitutes a philosophy antagonistic to all morality-based supernatural systems equally. For this reason, it may be considered an adversarial religion of sorts in that it purports to provide a system of belief whereby humans oppressed by ignorance may be liberated through the rejection of the primary tenets of their religion. Critics may argue that a philosophy should not be confused with religion, but the same argument is often abandoned in the face of Buddhism. The philosophical underpinnings of the latter have been - for lack of a better word - *religionized* by its apostles over the course of the last 2,500 years.

So, it is possible to consider Nietzschean atheism as an antagonistic religion - or at least, philosophy. But in the late nineteenth and twentieth century, there developed a strange child of this antagonistic strain which perhaps be called Adversarial Deism.

ADVERSARIAL DEISM

Islam and atheism are not the only adversarial spiritual traditions in the West.

Over the past 150 years, Nietzschean philosophy, calcified Christian institutions, burgeoning corporatism, urban blight, and post-industrial malaise provided fertile ground for a resurgence of fringe spiritual traditions that combined old pagan gods (or anti-gods) with idiosyncratic Gnostic sensibilities. In many ways, it was an outgrowth of nineteenth-century Romanticism. While many of today's practitioners' fashion themselves the Sons of Cain or the Daughters of the Moon, a good argument may be made that they are, in fact, more truly the Children of Rousseau. Yet this takes nothing away from the adversarial nature of their path, which uplifts a panoply of spiritual powers antagonistic toward the prevailing orthodox paradigm.*

---

* I am indebted to my good friend Shea Bile on this point, who first introduced me to the idea that contemporary adversarial spirituality is deeply indebted to the explosive philosophical writings of Friedrich Nietzsche.

Sometimes this antagonism is explicit: those who worship Lucifer, Satan, Lilith, Leviathan, or Cain - and any of their adjacent allies - are by very definition adversarial, since these are the Biblical enemies of the Abrahamic God. Others are less clear: Is being a Mormon an antagonistic stance? Do New Age angelology, Kabbalah, and ceremonial magic subjects attack the ruling paradigm, or are they simply mystic expressions of it? Reasonable minds may differ on these questions.

But more to our point: What of devotion and invocation of the Hellenic goddess Hekate? After all, her cult seems to grow daily. Is that path an adversarial one?

The question is more subtle than it seems and merits parsing. But in short: I believe it is - for the select few who practice Hekatean sorcery.

HEKATE THE ADVERSARY

Once you get past her contemporary gothic iconography, which definitely trends toward the Halloween-ish end of the spectrum, Hekate would *not* seem to be a good candidate for adversarial spirituality. After all - isn't she a Greek Goddess? And if (as I have said) Mediterranean paganism was never adversarial even in the final stages of its eradication, how can Hekate be the exception?

The answer to this relies upon the unique position Hekate holds in the spirituality of late antiquity. But even then, we must look past the surface. On the surface, Hekate is similar to other Greek gods and goddesses, all of which were non-binary powers capable of giving blessings or curses in equal measure, and Hekate was no different. Although, like other gods and goddesses, the earliest (and latest) descriptions of her nature focus primarily on her beneficial nature.

Many traditionalists point to the fact that the earliest description of Hekate's provenance and jurisdiction is also the most generous: Hesiod, a contemporary of Homer who lived in the eighth century BC, referred to Hekate in his *Theogony* as being gifted by Zeus, and holding triple jurisdiction over the earth, sea, and sky, and being "honored exceedingly by all the deathless gods."* He praises her as one who is invoked as a matter, of course, any time mortals make sacrifices or pray according to custom; one who grants honors and wealth to those whom she favors; one who sits beside "kings in judgment" and attends political assemblies. Hekate, says Hesiod, grants victory and glory both in sport and battle; grants success to horsemen, fishermen, shepherds, and farmers; and is a nurse to the young.†

From these associations, traditionalists argue with some force that a beloved and honored goddess who is a light-bringing torchbearer, who bestows favors of all kinds, nurtures maidens, and protects participants in the Eleusian Mysteries, is an unambiguously benevolent figure, and should be worshipped as such.‡ She would seem to be an unlikely vessel for adversarial expression.

All of which is true - up to a point.

But the following facts must be taken into account.

First, Hekate is not a goddess, but a Titan. She is the progeny of the primal, first-created beings: "For as many were born of

---

* Hesiod, *Theogony*, lines 410-452 (tr. H.G. Evelyn-White).
† Id.
‡ Many aspects of the Eleusian Mysteries are occluded to us even now, but a good glimpse at their structure may be found in Karl Kerenyi's *Eleusis* (Princeton University Press, 1991). In them, Hekate and Iakhos (Dionysus) serve as *dadoukhoi* (torchbearers) to guide the *mystai* to the initiation rites. Id. at 64. Hesiod's reference to Hekate as *kourotrophos* (nurse to the young) may be seen as an acknowledgement of her role as guard and guide in the Eleusian Mysteries.

Earth and Ocean, among these she has her due portion," says Hesiod.

Second, while the other Titans were enslaved by the gods, Hekate retained her jurisdiction. Unlike them, she may go where she wants, when she wants, and do what she wants. Again, Hesiod says that "she holds, as the division was at first from the beginning, privilege both in earth, and in heaven, and in the sea."

Third, her privilege in this regard seems to be due to the fact that she fought on the side of the gods against the Titans. She aided their rebellion against her own kind. In this way, she is a turncoat because she defied the bonds of blood to aid the gods' revolt and usher in a new age. It is no criticism to say so: Mortals may celebrate the bonds of blood we share with our kin, but to be bound by such ties is still to be bound, and Hekate, we are told, is *azostos* – unbound. She is literally unbound by restrictive clothing in the old depictions of her, which portray her in a loose-fitting chiton; she is unbound by the rule of the gods or the obligations to her Titanic kin; she is even unbound by the very bonds of fate that determine the destinies of every creature ever created and every spirit that exists.

Why is this?

The answer relates back to her true nature. Gods are the spirits who rule certain things; Titans are the things themselves. The god Poseidon rules the sea; the Titan Pontus *is* the sea. The god Apollo rules the sun; the Titan Helios *is* the sun. Like Pontus and Helios, Hekate is a Titan. So, if they are respectively the sea and the sun - then what is she?

What is Hekate?

The answer may be found in her associations. Each deity has certain things on earth - certain symbols - which are specifically associated with them. The Titan of the sun is associated with dawn, fire, frankincense, gold, lions, and laurel. Each of these is redolent of solar might. Aphrodite is associated with doves, shells, mirrors, apples, and copper.

Hekate, however, has her own associations. Her place in a home is the threshold, and in a city, its gate. Outside the city, she is found at the crossroads where three paths meet. Her hour is midnight. Her lunar phase the new moon. Her animal is the dog. Each of these has something in common. The threshold is neither in nor out of the house; it is the space between, just as the gate stands between what is in and out of the city. The crossroads is neither one road nor the other but the space between them. Midnight is the moment between one day and the next, just as the new moon is the dark night between lunar waxing and waning phases. And the dog had a particular function in ancient times, which was to guard the borders and boundaries between what was its master's property and what was not.

All of these associations point toward between-ness, to thresholds, to liminality - to the negative space that exists where the thing itself is not. I contend that Hekate is the very embodiment of these things. She is not a god, so she is not *over* thresholds. She is a Titan - so she *is* thresholds. She is the Between, and as such, she exists in the space between the city I live in and the city you live in; in the time between me writing this and the time that you read it; in the realm that lies between me when I shall have passed away, and you who shall outlive me. In all places, times, realms, dimensions, and internal and external states, she stands at the border, embodying the threshold: A gatekeeper who is a gate; a keykeeper who is a key; a torchbearer who is a torch.

In this regard, Hesiod's long description of her various jurisdictions now makes sense: Hekate decides who wins the athletic game because she is the threshold that the runner must cross. Hekate decides who wins the battle because she is the shield wall that either withstands or gives way beneath the assault. Hekate decides whether the child is born safely because she is the bodily threshold that the child must pass through to take its first breath.

And of course, it explains her role as psychopomp as well: after all, to descend into the underworld, a soul must make its *katabasis*, its descent, and pass through the Hadean gate though which none may return. Who better to escort the dead than one who is herself that very gate through which they pass? This may also explain her close affinity with Kerberos, the fierce guardian of that gate: both combine attributes of dogs, serpents, and triplicities. Both have a gatekeeper function, a hybrid form, and a monstrous nature.

MONSTRESS

For those who focus on Hekate's light-bringing nature, it may seem blasphemous to refer to her as monstrous. But the term must be defined:

The Oxford English Dictionary (OED) defines a monster primarily as a creature of myth which "combines elements of two or more animal forms, and is frequently of great size and ferocious appearance."

Hekate's size is indeterminate. In Hellenic art, she appears the same size of mortals, while on Roman coins, she is pictured as fairy-like, fitting onto the palm of Zeus' hand.* Yet a spell from Egypt calls her "giant."†

---

* Specifically, there is a Bactrian coin portraying on one side a diminutive torchbearing Hekate standing on the palm of Zeus' hand, and on the other Agathocles, who ruled an Alexandrian satrapy in what is now modern-day Afghanistan between 190 – 180 BCE.
† *The Greek Magical Papyri in Translation*, Ed. Hans Dieter Betz (Second Ed.), the University of Chicago Press, p. 89: PGM IV. 2714. Henceforth, PGM quotations shall be cited thus: PGM IV. 2714 (Betz, p. 89).

As for combining two or more animal forms, her imagery is replete with serpentine and canine references. Of her snakelike nature, the sorcerer of late antiquity conjured her thus:

> "[You] shake your locks
> Of fearful serpents on your brow, [you] who sound
> The roar of bulls out from your mouths, whose womb
> Is decked out with the scales of creeping things
> With poisonous rows of serpents down the back
> Bound down your backs with horrifying chains."*

Furthermore,

> "With scales of serpents are you dark;
> O you with hair of serpents, serpent girded,
> Who drink blood,
> Who bring death and destruction,
> And who feast on hearts, flesh-eater,
> Who devour those dead untimely
> And you who make grief resound and spread madness."†

And, too, Hekate is conjured as a "dog in maiden form,"‡ a grave-haunter who "feeds on filth"§ and "make[s] grief resound and spread[s] madness."**

The dog iconography is telling. While many think highly of dogs nowadays, it cannot be forgotten that in late antiquity the dog was a cemetery-prowling corpse-eater, and in Persian mysticism symbolized dangerous sub-lunar daimons.†† Furthermore, Hekate's stellar attribute was Sothis, the Dog

---

* PGM IV. 2800-2806 (Betz, p. 91).
† PGM IV. 2861-68 (Betz, p. 92).
‡ PGM IV. 2251 (Betz, p. 78).
§ PGM IV. 1402 (Betz, p. 65).
** PGM IV. 2867-68 (Betz, p. 92).
†† Sarah Iles Johnston, *Hekate Soteira*, Scholar's Press, 1990, p. 134-5

Star, which was thought to have a baneful effect, heralding in the season of contagion at summer's end.

Some of the attributions of Hekate in late antiquity, then, are clearly monstrous in the traditional sense. But the OED defines the term further: a monster can be "something extraordinary," a "prodigy," or "marvel," something which exhibits "an astonishing degree of excellence." Again, it is apropos: Her monstrosity is evinced in ancient texts by references to her unique power and potentiality.

In the Athannasakis translation of the Orphic Hymn to Hekate, she is actually referred to as "Monstrous Queen" (*amaimaketon basileian*). The root word is *maimao*: "to be eager, to quiver with eagerness." The "a" added to the beginning of the word inverts its meaning, rendering it un-eager; and it is close to a-machos: "can't be fought" or "implacable." The literal definition for *amaimaketos* is "irresistible" - yet even so it has monstrous connotations: the chimera, a fire-vomiting serpent/goat/lion hybrid, was described as *amaimaketon.**

In the very next line of the Orphic Hymn, she is referred to as "devouring wild beasts, ungirt and repulsive." Still, the full line in Greek is "*therobromon azoston, aprosmakon eidos ekousan,*" a more literal translation of which is "heralded by wild beasts, ungirt, irresistible of form."† And indeed, *aprosomakon eidos ekousan* literally means "not-fighting-against-form-having."‡ Inherent in the epithet is a sense of being embodied, of being immanent, apprehendable - which may have infernal connotations, since, by the standards of Platonic philosophy, the more formless something was, the more pure and celestial;

---

* Many thanks to my astute friend T. Susan Chang for providing insight into the etymology of these words. Susan's erudite and accessible writings on tarot divination can be found at www.tsusanchang.com.
† Id.
‡ Id.

whereas the more it had shape, dimensions, and form, the more non-celestial or sub-lunar it was - and therefore "lower:" more available to mortals; less godlike.*

So: If Hekate "did not resist having form" and was considered "irresistible," what form did she have? And what irresistible function did she actually perform?

Spiritual encounters are, of course, subjective, but they are informed by cultural influences. Most Athenians would have encountered Hekate directly through the Eleusian Mysteries. This ancient ten-day psychodrama drew thousands of participants annually to Eleusis, ten miles outside of Athens. It provided devotees with an opportunity to experience first-hand the myth of Persephone and Demeter by re-enacting the Mother's mournful search (and joyous recovery) of her lost Daughter. After days of fasting, dancing, singing, and drinking the mind-altering *kykeon*, initiates would have acted out a descent to the underworld where it is more than likely that an actor portraying Hekate would have defended them from other actors threatening them in the guise of malicious infernal spirits.

While Hekate's staged intervention was presumably welcomed by the frightened initiates, the very fact that she was invoked to dispel such infernal threats implies not that she was *opposed* to infernal powers but that she was closely *associated* with them.

Comparisons abound. In Egypt, the apotropaic god was Bes - the squat, bearded, ithyphallic, and ostrich-plumed demon-

---

* Johnston, p. 122 (stating, "Platonic doctrine taught that the incorporeal was closer to divinity than the corporeal; embodiment was the mark of the hylic world"). Johnston discusses Iamblichus' contention in *On the Mysteries of Egypt* to the effect that "angels, archangels and gods are all simple in form or formless, whereas daemones, heroes, and souls take on more complex, specific shapes." Id.

king whose idol adorned the women's quarters to frighten away his subordinate demons.* An identical function was held by Pazuzu in Babylonian culture: the avian arch-demon was installed in the home to keep away the horde of lower demons that might otherwise work mischief.† And in archaic Greece, the omnipresent gorgoneion - with its bulging eyes, protruding tongue, and fang-bearing grimace - graced pendants and shields alike, to ward off harmful spirits and enemy soldiers. Similar to Bes and Pazuzu, the gorgon is an arch-demon that scares off lower demons, as cats deter mice. And Hekate, with her "scaled womb" and "locks of fearful serpents," was clearly gorgon-adjacent.‡

Here, of course, it must be acknowledged that the gods of Greece, in general, were non-binary and had various aspects and emanations which embodied different (and even opposing) principles in ways that may seem paradoxical to us now. And different people would have been drawn to different aspects of the same deity.

For instance, well-educated students of philosophy would most likely be drawn to the Hekate of the Chaldean Oracles - the formless, fiery creatrix who proceeded from the demiurge and imbued all sentient beings with a soul.

Most people in Hellenic and Roman times were not, of course, well-educated philosophy students, but rather farmers, fishers, merchants, soldiers, and sailors - and these would have simply known Hekate as the frightening but useful spirit which drove away devils at Eleusis, or cured their mania at her

---

* Geraldine Pinch, *Magic in Ancient Egypt*, Univ. of Texas Press (1994), p. 44 & 171.
† See, for example, the Sumerian declaration: "I am Pazuzu, son of Hanbu, king of the evil phantoms / I ascended the mighty mountain that quaked/ the winds that I went against were headed toward the West / One by one I broke their wings." Benjamin R. Foster, *Before the Muses*, Third Ed., CDL Press (2005), p. 178. "Winds" are synonymous with evil spirits, in this context.
‡ PGM IV. 2800-28004 (Betz, p. 91).

shrines in Samothrace or Aegina.* Accordingly, they would have left her small food offerings at crossroads during the new moon so that she would ward off restless ghosts. Such citizens were naturally participating in the state cult, not rejecting it. There is no argument that Hekatean worship among philosophers or simple devotees was adversarial.

But the same cannot be said for the sorcerers of late antiquity - for whom there was a Hekate that was quite, quite different from the one found in Chaldean Oracles or Eleusian Mysteries.

BLACK DOG

In our day and age, when nearly every neopagan in the West declares themselves to be a witch, wizard, mage, or priest, it is hard to grasp that in ancient times, this was not the case. In the archaic, classical, and post-classical age, most pagans (as is the case with Christians, Jews, and Muslims today) were mere devotees, whose levels of devotion ran the gamut from enthusiastic to grudging. Of these devotees, there would have been a small priestly class whose members were employed by the state - be it polis or empire - to carry out the regular calendar of ritual work and temple maintenance that was native to their local cult. These were the recognized spiritual leaders of villages, towns, and cities.†

---

* Sorita d'Este, *Circle for Hekate: Vol. 1: History & Mythology*, Avalonia (2017), p. 103 & 116.

† Interestingly, priesthood as a class was not consistent throughout the Mediterranean: While Near-Eastern and Egyptian priesthood was treated as a sacred guild with millenia of traditions, religion in Greece was (almost) priest-less, in that with the exception of the major shrines (Eleusis, Delphi, Dodona, etc), most officiants of sacrifice and ceremony during the Greek calendar year were regular citizens elected by the elders of the local polis based on their income and standing. Walter Burkert, *Greek Religion*, Harvard Univ. Press (1985), p. 95-8 (stating "Greek religion might almost be called a religion without priests: there is no priestly caste as a closed group

But there was a type of spiritual practitioner in no way authorized by the priestly class or paid for by the state. This type was a spirit-worker for hire (often itinerant) who was regarded with contempt by the authorities and fear by the populace - and for good reason. Working outside the established system, these practitioners (for the right price) would perform rituals to remove (or send) hexes, exorcise demons, increase luck, fix chariot-races, rig trials, bless friends, curse enemies, silence slander, change indifference to desire, heal the sick or sicken the healthy. They often offered astrological insight too and claimed the ability to divine destinies, predict futures, and receive prophetic dreams. They sold protective amulets and phylacteries, as well as curse-tablets and various salves, oils, potions, and products guaranteeing everything from second-sight to invisibility. The selling of such services was almost always illegal, and in late antiquity, the punishment for doing so was crucifixion or immolation.[*]

And yet, this despised art - and its despised artists - persisted. Their clients seem to have been mostly those living at the margins of society, whose lives were filled with uncertainty, and who were desperate to improve their odds to survive and thrive in a dangerous world. Strange as it may seem to us today, the clients themselves risked death to engage the services of a sorcerer.

Did they get value for their money, for the risk they took? We can only conjecture. But the near-universal fear of such

---

with fixed tradition, education, initiation, and hierarchy, and even in the permanently established cults there is no *disciplina*, but only usage, *nomos*." Id. at 95.

[*] Daniel Ogden, *Magic, Witchcraft, and Ghosts in the Greek and Roman Worlds*, Oxford Univ. Press (2002), p. 279 (quoting Pseudo-Paulus' opinions on Sulla's law of 81 BCE: "Those who perform or direct the performance of impious or nocturnal rites, in order to bewitch, bind, or tie a person, are either crucified or thrown to the beasts... Actual mages, however, are burned alive").

practitioners speaks to the widely-held belief that their methods were effective.

But what were their methods?

The record we have comes from several long Christian rants, a few fragmentary Roman novels and Greek plays, numerous curse tablets found in graves, caves, and wells, and a trove of documents from Thebes containing several hundred actual conjurations written for and by working sorcerers in Roman Egypt. These documents, which are known collectively as the Greek Magical Papyri (PGM), are by far the most reliable proof we have of how sorcery was actually performed in late antiquity.

What they reveal is this: if hired to do so, these outlaw sorcerers would have invoked one of several mediating gods to aid their clients through a strange mix of devotional hymns and compulsive techniques. The gods called upon to perform this virulent strain of outlaw magic are an odd lot, ranging from Anubis to Apollo - but Hekate was one of the foremost.

The reason for this is simple: much sorcery in late antiquity had nothing to do with energy or wish-fulfillment; it was ghost magic. It required ghosts to work - and not just any sort of ghost, but *auroi* - restless spirits of mortals who died under unfortunate circumstances, either untimely, or by violence, or while uninitiated, unmarried, or unburied. The spirits of such unfortunate ones, it was presumed, did not immediately enter Hades, but roamed the upper world restlessly, jealous of the living and furious over their fates, and were therefore vulnerable to those of a sorcerous persuasion. But to persuade such restless spirits, a mediator was needed - and not just any mediator, but a soul guide or *psychopomp*. And the pre-eminent *psychopomps* in late antiquity were Hekate, Hermes, and Anubis. Of these three, the most commonly invoked soul guide - particularly for baneful workings - was Hekate. In the PGM, she is the unrivaled queen of necromancy, which is as much as to say the queen of adversarial sorcery.

ADVERSARIAL SORCERY

Sorcery is inherently adversarial. This may seem at first to be nonsense because even a superficial review of the spells from late antiquity shows that most begin by calling upon the gods, and their success depends upon gods' compliance. How then can the sorcerer's work be deemed antagonistic to the very system on which it depends?

The answer lies within the unique methodology of sorcery in Roman Egypt, which is not (like the Orphic Hymns) devotional, but *compulsive*. Divine compliance with mortal desires is repeatedly *compelled* through the use of barbarous names, mystic formulas, recitation of the seven sacred vowels, threat narratives, success narratives, and above all by *theosis*: what may be called the assumption of the god face.

The god face technique is a means of compelling a god by becoming a god. When using it, the sorcerer abandons her own identity. She is no longer Jane This or Joan That. Instead, she declares that she is the hyper-cosmic demiurge (creator/craftsman) of the world. And because the demiurge created all reality, now the sorcerer may do the same: she can un-create and re-create reality since she and he are one:

> "Come to me,
> You from the four winds, Ruler of All,
> Who breathed spirit into men for life,
> Whose is the hidden and unspeakable Name -
> It cannot be uttered by human mouth....
> Come to my mind and my understanding for all the time of my life,
> And accomplish for me all the desires of my soul!
> For you are I, and I am you.
> Whatever I say must happen
> For I have your name as a unique phylactery in my heart,
> And no flesh, though moved, will overpower me;

No spirit will stand against me -
Neither daimon nor visitation nor any other of the evil beings of Hades,
Because of your Name, which I have in my soul and invoke."*

This self-identification is transformative and grants the sorcerer hyper-cosmic authority and demiurgic power. By taking on the mask of the primal creator - by fully declaring and embodying it - the sorcerer can influence the gods themselves to work her will: an act that is unquestionably adversarial.

But why is working one's will adversarial?

BENDING THE MOIRA'S THREADS

Here the modern mind encounters a cultural gulf that is nearly uncrossable because we in the West are used to thinking that the life we live is the direct result of the choices we make. We constantly celebrate our free will - the choice to do *what* we want, *when* we want, in the *way* we want. Our fate, we believe, is in our hands. Indeed, Christianity's entire underpinnings rely upon this idea: if you use your free will to have faith in Christ, you are saved and go to heaven; if you use your free will to disavow Christ, you are damned and go to hell. Everything depends upon your decision, and your decision is the expression of your will.

This concept of choice pervades our entire culture. And even for those who consider themselves atheists, being raised in a Christian (or post-Christian) culture still creates a superstructure in the mind. This conceptual framework elevates this concept of free will, of choice, of choosing your destiny, of being *in charge.*

---

* PGM XIII. 760-795 (Betz, p. 190-91).

But citizens in Roman Egypt did not for a moment imagine that they were *in charge* or that they would get to choose their destiny. Their destiny had been chosen for them by powers older and greater than the gods themselves.

Those born into an Egyptian tradition believed that the Seven Hathors visited each child on the seventh night after its birth to announce its predetermined fate.* Those with a Hellenic background revered the Fates, known as the three Moirae ("Shares"): Klotho, Lakhesis, Atropos. They believed that these three primordial feminine powers spun, measured, and cut the thread of life so as to predetermine each mortal's destiny.

In short: everyone had a fate, and that fate was not only predetermined but unalterable. Not only did you have no choice in deciding what sort of family you were born into, or whether you were short or tall, but the Moirae had already determined your personality, your skills, your opportunities, your challenges, your choices, and your outcomes: whether you married or were single, whether your ventures prospered or failed, whether you were healthy or sick, died young or old, were remembered or forgotten. And since life was bitter for many, the phrase "bitter necessity" was used to describe this predetermined system of suffering.

In time, Necessity (Ananke) was acknowledged as a goddess in her own right and one whose inescapable and implacable yoke led mortals helplessly from one misfortune to the next, from the cradle to the grave.†

There were two hedges against this misery. The first was devotion, and the second was sorcery.

---

* Pinch, Geraldine, *Magic in Ancient Egypt*, University of Texas Press (1995) p. 56.
† But over time, certain philosophers began to suggest that mortals might have some say in their lives. Epicurus may have been the first to articulate the idea that "some things happen of necessity, others by chance, others through our own agency."

Devotion consisted of piety and prayers, by which devotees begged the gods to spare them the worst aspects of their predetermined fates. But there was a logical disconnect with such prayers. After all, *the gods themselves were considered subject to the Moirae.* The gods themselves were said to be born, live, and in some cases die, and they had certain strengths, weaknesses, successes, and failures - all predetermined by the Fates, which were older than them and would ultimately outlast them. An old saying ran, *Mortals fear the gods; gods fear the Fates.**

So, if mortal lives were dictated by the Fates, how could gods improve them? The quandary was epitomized by the Roman Emperor Tiberius, who believed so completely in astrological destiny that he neglected to supplicate the gods because it could do no possible good.

Sorcery, however, was a different matter. Although sorcery could incorporate preliminary hymns and prayers, the dark heart of the dark art was something entirely different. Through the technology of sorcery, the ritualist took on the godface and stepped into the shoes of the demiurge himself, becoming a co-creator in her own right, bending the skeins of fate to improve the destiny of herself (or her clients). And what can be more adversarial than that - than treading on the toes of those who control the very gods; by declaring ourselves to be the primal power that begets reality itself; by stealing fire from heaven?

---

* The concept is neatly summed up by this exchange from Aeschylus' play Prometheus Bound:
> "Chorus : Who then is the helmsman of Ananke (Necessity)?
> Prometheus : The three-shaped (Fates) and mindful Erinyes (Furies).
> Chorus : Can it be that Zeus has less power than they do?
> Prometheus : Yes, in that even he cannot escape what is foretold."
> *Aeschylus, Prometheus Bound 515 ff (trans. Weir Smyth) (Greek tragedy C5th B.C.)*

Well and good, perhaps: but how do we know that this is actually how ancient sorcery works?

We know because *it is written explicitly into the conjurations of the PGM.* And what we find in those two-millennia-old conjurations is nothing less than a recipe for rebelling against Fate.

FATEBREAKER

Hekate, paradoxically, is presented in the PGM as both *being* Fate, being *subject* to Fate, and *defying* Fate. She is thus intrinsic to this type of sorcery.

In the PGM's "Prayer to Selene for Any Spell," the ritualist says unequivocally of Hekate-Selene: "You are Justice, and the Moira's threads - Klotho, Lakhesis, Atropos."*

Likewise, in the "Document to the Waning Moon," the sorcerer cries to Hekate-Selene:

> "Night, Darkness, broad Chaos, Necessity hard to
> escape are you!
> You're Moira and Erinys, torment, Justice and
> Destroyer[.]"†

In that same rite, Hekate-Selene is called the "Spinner of Fate" - clearly conflating her with Klotho, the Fate who spins mortal destinies on her cosmic spindle.

And yet, after acknowledging that "awesome Destiny is ever subject to you," the ritualist urges Hekate: "Thrice bound goddess, set free yourself!" The concept of being thrice-bound most likely references Hekate as being *bound* by each of the

---

* PGM IV. 2795-96 (Betz, p. 90)
† PGM IV. 2860 (Betz, p. 92)

three Fates - and yet being capable of *unbinding* her triple bonds - with the sorcerer's help.

But to what end? Once free, Hekate-Selene, the "Ruler of Tartaros," is a bid to "whirl up out of the darkness and subvert all things" - meaning that she may unweave the skein of Fate to do the sorcerer's bidding. In that particular spell, she is adjured to alter destiny by utterly destroying the sorcerer's enemy.* Hekate has the power to un-make and re-make destiny, we are told, for the hymn states, "Klotho will spin out her threads for you."†

Thus, in just a few lines, Hekate-Selene is said to *be* one of the Fates, to be *bound* by the Fates, to be capable of *breaking* the bonds of Fate, and to be able to *direct* the workings of Fate. These are, of course, all contradictory, but in the paganism of late antiquity, contradiction is the hallmark of divinity.

So: Hekate is intrinsic to the adversarial process of un-weaving and re-weaving Fate. Now, the important is the question - What is the sorcerer's role in all this?

The answer is simple: *She frees Hekate to do so.*

How does she do this? Ironically, *by binding Hekate to her will.*

It is a great paradox: Hekate is freed through subjugation. But how to subjugate a goddess? How to bind an eternal, ineffable, ubiquitous Titan? The PGM is clear on this point: *By using the arcane knowledge bestowed on the sorcerer by the demiurge himself in order to become the demiurge himself.*

The text in the PGM's "Mithras Rite" is explicit; in it, the sorcerer conjures the hyper-cosmic demiurge, saying:

"[B]e not angry at my potent chants

---

* PGM IV. 2243-44 (Betz, p. 78).
† PGM IV. 2248 (Betz, p. 78).

For you, yourself arranged these things among
mankind
For them to learn about the threads of the Moirai,
And thus, with your advice, I call your name: HORUS
Which is in a number equivalent to those of the Moirai:
AKHAIPHO THOTHO PHIAKHA AIE EIA IAE EIA
THOTHO PHIAKHA."*

The meaning is straightforward: The sorcerer has been gifted
by the demiurge with the ability to learn how Fate may be
thwarted, and it is her birthright to use that gift. In doing so,
she defies the circumstances of her birth by declaring her
theosis - her godface - thus acknowledging the immanence of
the divine within herself, with all the power that attains:

"I, born mortal, from mortal womb,
But transformed by tremendous power and an
incorruptible right hand
And with immortal spirit
The immortal AION
And Master of the Fiery Diadems;
I, sanctified through holy consecrations,
While there subsists within me, holy, for a short time,
My human soul-might,
Which I will again receive after the present bitter and
relentless Necessity
Which is pressing down upon me."†

The "bitter and relentless Necessity" is the sorcerer's destiny:
The family she was born into, the genes that she inherited, the
circumstances of her upbringing, the deprivations and injuries
she experienced, and the restrictions imposed upon her by her
gender, race, sexuality, appearance, and mental and emotional
capacities. These she does not deny. Indeed, it is because of
them that she undergoes "holy consecration" to receive
"immortal   soul-might"   that   she   might   ultimately   be

---

* PGM IV. 453-457 (Betz, p. 46).
† PGM IV. 516-526 (Betz, p. 48) .

"transformed by tremendous power and an incorruptible right hand / And with immortal spirit" to manifest herself through theosis as the godface of immortal Aion: the lion-faced scion of eternity and initiation. In essence, she is becoming the master of Necessity - *indeed, its very consort*, for in the Orphic Hymns, one of Aion's avatars is Chronos (Time), "a serpentine being with the heads of a lion, a man, and bull, whose consort was Ananke (Inevitability)."*

Thus, being the consort of Necessity gives the sorcerer influence over Necessity; and by declaring the same, the sorcerer may compel even the gods themselves to alter her Fate:

"Come, Master-God!
And tell me – by Necessity – concerning this matter:
For I am the one who revolted against you!"†

There are multiple techniques for turning Necessity against the gods. Still, the most common is the recitation of the *voces magicae*: the "inutterable names" of the gods, in which they delight, and by which they are compelled:

"I have spoken your [names]!
Therefore, lord, do [such and such] by Necessity, lest I shake heaven."‡

The threat is real because the names themselves are nonsensical, inhuman, eternal – a sort of daimonic language

---

* A clear conflation between Kronos and Aion can be found in the *Orphic Theogonies*, which describe a spirit named Chronos (Time), a serpentine being with the heads of a lion, a man and a bull, whose consort was Ananke (Inevitability). This primordial couple cracked open the "egg" of the universe with their coils, and then encircled all of the kosmos like a double Oroboros. *Orphic Theogonies*, collected by Otto Kern, lines 53 – 86.
† PGM IV. 3109 (Betz, p. 98).
‡ PGM III. 538 (Betz, p. 31).

that replicates the original utterance of the demiurge which begat all created beings of the seen and unseen worlds:

> "[O]n account of the pressing and bitter and inexorable Necessity,
> I invoke the immortal names, living and honored,
> Which never pass into mortal nature and are not declared
> In articulate speech by human tongue or mortal speech or mortal sound."*

The utterance of the *voces magicae* binds the gods fast; they "must not escape" the string of names, vowels, and correspondences, both mythic and phenomenal. A breathtaking example of a sorcerous compulsion of Hekate-Selene from the PGM runs as follows:†

> "Mare! Kore! Dragoness! Lamp! Lightning Flash!
> Star! Lion! She-Wolf! AEO EE
> A sieve, an old utensil, is my symbol,
> And one morsel of flesh, a piece of coral,
> Blood of a turtledove, hoof of a camel,
> Hair of a virgin cow, the seed of Pan...
> A gray-eyed woman's body with legs outspread,
> A black sphinx's pierced vagina:
> All of these are the symbol of my power.
> The bond of all necessity will be sundered....
> The Moirai throw away your endless thread,
> Unless you check my magic's winged shaft,
> Swiftest to reach the mark. For to escape
> The fate of my words is impossible:
> Happen, it must. Don't force yourself to hear
> The symbols forward and then in reverse again!
> You will, willy-nilly, do what's needed!
> Ere useless light becomes your fate,
> Do what I say, O Maid, Ruler of Tartaros!

---

* PGM IV. 605-610 (Betz, p. 50).
† PGM IV. 2301 (Betz, p. 79).

I've bound your pole with Kronos' chains,
And with awesome compulsion, I hold fast your thumb.
Tomorrow does not come unless my will is done!"*

This astonishing declaration reveals the true extent of the sorcerer's power: having called forth the godhood in herself, she reverses the wheel of fortune so that it binds the very gods themselves, who must then obey her charge or be deprived of existence! She is no longer bound: *they* are bound by the chains of Kronos (Time) and the "awesome compulsion" of Necessity.

It is worth noting that it is not always Aion or Kronos that the sorcerer identifies as through the process of theosis; indeed, in the syncretic spirituality of late antiquity, the hyper-cosmic demiurge goes by many names. Sometimes he is Aion, sometimes Ra, sometimes Helios, sometimes Thoth, sometimes Iao (the Hellenized name for YHVH). But always his essence is the power behind all other powers, the true source of Necessity:

"I conjure you in the Hebrew tongue,
And by virtue of the Necessity of the Necessitators:
.....Hitherto me, O greatest in heaven,
For whom the heaven has come into being as a dancing place
SATIS PHPHQOOUTH HQRA OITKHOU
Of Necessity perform [such and such deed]."†

This demiurge has no true identity because identity is inherently limiting: if you are this, you cannot be that; if you are him, you cannot be her. The demiurge is beyond all limit, so it is beyond all description. But since language cannot encompass an indescribable force, the spells themselves conjure this unspeakable being by a series of paradoxical and contradictory names. At times this primordial power is even invoked as the god-killing beast Typhon:

---

* PGM IV. 2302 – 2322 (Betz, p. 79-80).
† PGM III. 129 – 131 (Betz, p. 21-22).

"Typhon, in hours unlawful and unmeasured,
You who've walked on unquenched, clear-crackling fire
You who are over snows, below dark ice,
You who hold sovereignty over the Moirai,
I invoked you in prayer, I call, almighty one."*

This hyper-cosmic overgod has sovereignty over the Moirae/Fates. By assuming his mantle, by stealing his crown, the sorcerer can command not only the gods beneath the demiurge but the lower spirits beneath the gods: those infinite cohorts of invisible beings who animate the celestial, aerial, and chthonic realms, carrying out the business of the material world. These servants are the "sunless ones" who "send Fate" to chain mortals to their destinies:†

"O masters of all the living and dead,
O heedful in many necessities of gods and men,
O concealers of things now seen,
O directors of Nemesis who spend every hour with you,
O senders of Fate who travel around the whole world,
O commanders of the rulers,
O exalters of the abased,
O revealers of the hidden!"‡

These "masters," "directors," and "commanders," are akin to the decans who rule the material plane from the 36 quadrants of the Zodiac; they are akin to the dukes of hell in Renaissance grimoires who command legions of infernal servants. By commanding them, the sorcerer commands the servants themselves; she conjures these "bringers of compulsion" who are:

"Shudderful fighters, fearful ministers,

---

* PGM IV. 268-272 (Betz, p. 43).
† PGM IV. 1331-89 (Betz, p. 63-4).
‡ PGM XII. 218-221 (Betz, p. 161).

Turning the spindle, freezing snow and rain, air-
traversers,
Causing summer heat, wind-bringers,
Lords of Fate, inhabitants of dark Erebos,
Bringers of compulsion, sending flames of fire,
Bringing snow and dew, wind-releasers,
Disturbers of the deep, treaders on the calm sea, mighty
in courage,
Grievers of the heart, powerful potentates, cliff-
walkers,
Adverse daimons, iron-hearted, wild-tempered, unruly,
Guarding Tartaros, misleading Fate, all-seeing, all-
hearing, all-subjecting
Heaven-walkers, spirit-givers, living simply, heaven-
shakers."*

So, then: these "Lords of Fate" who are charged with
implementing the dictates of Fate, may be turned by their
handlers to "mislead Fate" and "shake heaven" by "bringing
compulsion" as dictated by the sorcerer who speaks through
the godface of the eternal Aion or inexorable Iao or terrible
Typhon.

This magic breaks the chains of Necessity; indeed, it "subverts
all things," converting the implacable Seven Hathors into the
seven compliant asp-faced virgins who greet the sorcerer as a
sister and subject themselves to her will.†

---

* PGM. IV. 1356-1363 (Betz, p. 64).
† PGM IV. 662-670 (Betz, p. 51): "After saying this, see the doors
thrown open, and seven virgins come from deep within, dressed
linen, with the faces of asps. These are the Fates of Heaven, and wield
golden wands. Seeing them, greet them with these words: Hail, O
seven Fates of heaven, O noble and good virgins / O sacred ones and
companions of MINIMIRRORPHOR /O most holy guardians of the
four pillars!"

But integral to this magic is the presence of a spirit mediator. In the magic of late antiquity, Hekate is the mediator *par excellence*, for she alone is identified as being the Fates, their instrumentality, and their compeller. She is *epiphanistate* - the "most manifest one." Her epiphany is the dog, and - being "a dog in maiden form" - she comes when called.

But how to call her? How do we make the mediator manifest?

Here, the sources agree. The process is not difficult. Offerings left at the crossroad during the full moon attract her like a moth to a flame - hymns spoken to her by night can win her attention. The recital of her epithets from the Orphic Hymns or PGM establishes the sorcerer's credentials. The articulation of her specific associations, secret names, and *voces magicae* gain her compliance; and the sorcerer's formal declaration of her theosis by assuming the godface of the demiurge gives her the authority to free Hekate by binding her, and so begin the process of un-weaving and re-weaving the very skein of Fate.

That this process is adversarial in the deepest sense cannot be denied. That Hekate is integral to it is apparent. That the sorcerers who engage on such a level with the powers of the cosmos are few and far between is very likely. And yet, she who dares to do so gains not only the greatest ally imaginable but experiences the ecstasy of transforming her own destiny and becoming a co-creator capable of altering the very fabric of reality.

Hekate thus may be a staunch ally to those who walk the adversarial path. And in doing so, she can provide access to a traditional current of ancient magic that flows uninterrupted from Roman Egypt to our own day and age. It is true that it is not a compliant, humble, and safe path. It is a path for those who are dissatisfied with their fates, whose prayers have fallen on deaf ears, who are unafraid to claim sovereignty with the gods themselves by taking up the sword of sorcery and severing the bonds that bind both Hekate and themselves in order to re-order their world.

Indeed, they have no choice: their hearts cry to be unfettered by Fate; their souls yearn to ascend (and descend) to heights (and depths) unknown; their spirits are fiercely independent; their minds revolt against the chains of oppression; their bodies rebel against the bonds that bind them.

Such seekers as these will not allow the spiritual and material encroachments of our strange age to continue without resistance, for their very natures run contrary to the idea of outside rule; their eyes glare at their handlers with hostility; their muscles strain fiercely against their bonds.

And their voices, like Moloch's, are for open war.

Recommended Reading

Sorita d'Este & David Rankine: *Hekate Liminal Rites: A Study of the rituals, magic and symbols of the torch-bearing Triple Goddess of the Crossroads*

Sorita d'Este: *Hekate: Keys to the Crossroads*

Sorita d'Este: *Circle for Hekate - Volume I: History & Mythology*

Jack Grayle: *The Hekataeon*

Cyndi Brannen: *Entering Hekate's Garden: The Magick, Medicine & Mystery of Plant Spirit Witchcraft*

Stephen Ronan: *The goddess Hekate (Studies in ancient pagan and Christian religion & philosophy)*

The Greek Magical Papyri in Translation Edited by Hans Dieter Betz

Sarah Iles Johnston: *Hekate Soteira: A Study of Hekate's Roles in the Chaldean Oracles and Related Literature*

Demetra George: *Mysteries of the Dark Moon: The Healing Power of the Dark Goddess*

Temple of Ascending Flame

Temple of Ascending Flame is a platform for individuals around the world who want to share certain aspects of their work with the Draconian current with other adepts of the path and for those who simply need guidance into Draconian self-initiatory magic. It is both for newcomers who make their first steps on the Path of the Dragon and for experienced individuals who wish to progress on the Left Hand Path. We are not a "magical order." We do not charge fees for membership and our work is not based on any hierarchies. There are no restrictions on participation in our open projects, and in our inner work we welcome all who are capable of receiving and channeling the Gnosis of the Dragon.

More information: **ascendingflame.com**
Contact: **info@ascendingflame.com**

RITES OF LUCIFER

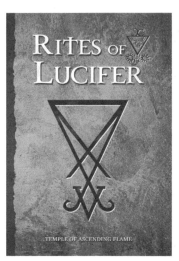

Lucifer is the archetype of the Adversary, initiator and guide on the Path of the Nightside. He is the fallen angel of Christian legends, the Devil of witches' Sabbats, one of primal Draconian Gods, Demon Prince of the Air, and Infernal Emperor of old grimoires. The purpose of this book is to delve into his initiatory role on the Draconian Path through chosen masks and manifestations which Lucifer has used over the ages to reveal his presence to mankind, bestowing his blessings on Initiates and scourging the ignorant. Essays and rituals included here explore both his bright and dark aspects, the face of the Light Bearer and the horned mask of the Devil.

Light and Darkness in Luciferian Gnosis by Asenath Mason - **The Light Bearer Ritual** by Temple of Ascending Flame - **Invocation of the Dark Initiator** by Temple of Ascending Flame - **The Mind of Lucifer** by Rev Bill Duvendack - **Purifying Fire (The Seed of Luciferian Gnosis)** by Edgar Kerval - **Lord of the Air** by Temple of Ascending Flame - **Lucifer - The Trickster** by Daemon Barzai - **The Shadow Companion** by Temple of Ascending Flame - **Holographic Luciferianism** by Rev Bill Duvendack - **The Adversarial Current of Lucifer** by Asenath Mason - **Invocation of the Adversary** by Temple of Ascending Flame - **Freedom through Death** by Cristian Velasco - **Emperor of Shadow and Light** by Pairika Eva Borowska - **The God of Witchcraft** by Temple of Ascending Flame - **The Infernal Spirit of Old Grimoires** by Temple of Ascending Flame - **Masks of Lucifer Ritual** by Rev Bill Duvendack

ISBN-10: 1505295092
ISBN-13: 978-1505295092

VISIONS OF THE NIGHTSIDE

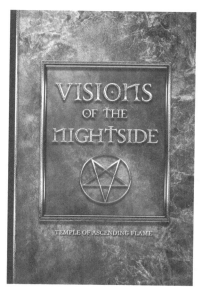

Collection of essays, rituals and various expressions of personal gnosis written by members and associates of the Temple of Ascending Flame. Unique and evocative in its content, the book comprises powerful manifestations of magical practice with the forces of the Nightside: dark gods and goddesses, primal energies of the Void, entities residing in the Qliphothic Tree of Death, demons of infernal regions, and spirits from a whole range of traditions. Compiled and edited by Asenath Mason, it is a practical research and insight into the magic of the Left Hand Path within the modern context, with contributions from working magicians and initiates of the Draconian Tradition.

Gnosis of the Void by Asenath Mason - **Setnacht** by Frater Eremor - **Hecate: Blessed Mother of Witches** by Pairika-Eva Borowska - **Mea Magna Mater Hecate. My Immersion in Multicolored Blackness** by Selene-Lilith - **Night on Bald Mountain: An Introduction to Slavic Witchcraft** by Febosfer - **Invocation to Lilith** by Asenath Mason - **Into the Void** by Frater GS - **Echoes** by Rev Bill Duvendack - **Ravens of Dispersion** by Asenath Mason - **Poseidon's Trident** by Rev Bill Duvendack - **Invocation of Sekhmet** by Asenath Mason - **The Lady of the Flame** by Asenath Mason - **Lucifer's Trident Ritual** by Rev Bill Duvendack - **Whispers From The Void (Exploration of Baratchial through the 12th Tunnel)** by Edgar Kerval - **Demeter: Draconian Goddess** by Fr. Nephilim

ISBN-10: 150865834X
ISBN-13: 978-1508658344

TREE OF QLIPHOTH

Tree of Qliphoth is our third anthology, exploring the dark side of the Qabalistic Tree as a map of Draconian Initiation. In essays, rituals and other expressions of personal research and experience, magicians and initiates of the Draconian Tradition discuss the realms of the Nightside, teachings and gnosis of its dark denizens, as well as practical methods developed both within the Temple and through their individual work. Material included in this book will give the reader a foretaste of these forces and a glimpse of what you can expect while embarking on the self-initiatory journey through the labyrinths of the Dark Tree.

Lilith by Temple of Ascending Flame - **In the Cave of Lilith** by Asenath Mason - **Naamah** by S.TZΣ. Swan - **Gates of Naamah** by M King - **The Dark Tower** by Calia van de Reyn - **Gamaliel** by Temple of Ascending Flame - **Lilith and Samael** by Asenath Mason & Rev Bill Duvendack - **Samael** by Temple of Ascending Flame - **Invocation of Adrammelech** by Rev Bill Duvendack - **Poisoned Well** by Rev Bill Duvendack - **A'arab Zaraq** by Temple of Ascending Flame - **Invocation of the Dark Venus** by Asenath Mason - **Invocation of Baal** by Rev Bill Duvendack - **Niantiel Working** by Asenath Mason - **Thagirion** by Temple of Ascending Flame - **Invocation of Belphegor** by Asenath Mason - **Invocation of Sorath** by Asenath Mason - **Thagirion** by Pairika-Eva Borowska - **The Cave of Lafcursiax** by Edgar Kerval - **The Qabalism of Lucifer's Sigil** by Rev Bill Duvendack - **Golachab** by Temple of Ascending Flame - **Invocation of Asmodeus** by Christiane Kliemannel - **Invocation of the King of the Nine Hells** by Rev Bill Duvendack - **Nine Hells of Asmodeus** by Asenath Mason - **Gha'agsheblah** by Temple of Ascending Flame - **Invocation of Astaroth** by Christiane Kliemannel - **Seven Gates of the Underworld** by Asenath Mason - **The Abyss** by Temple of Ascending Flame - **Invocation of Choronzon** by Rev Bill Duvendack - **Invocation of Shugal** by Rev Bill Duvendack - **Invocation of the Beast of the Abyss** by Rev Bill Duvendack - **Opening the Gates of Choronzon to Sitra Ahra** by Zeis Araújo - **Itzpapalotl** by N.A:O - **Ritual of Babalon** by Asenath Mason - **Satariel** by Temple of Ascending Flame - **Invocation of Lucifuge** by Christiane Kliemannel - **Summoning of the Lord of the Night** by Rev Bill Duvendack - **The Spider and the Web of Fates** by Asenath Mason & Pairika-Eva Borowska - **Ghagiel** by Temple of Ascending Flame - **Invocation of Beelzebub** by Christiane Kliemannel - **Litany to the Lord of the Flies** by Rev Bill Duvendack - **Experiencing the Strength of Belial** by Mafra Lunanigra - **Thaumiel** by Temple of Ascending Flame - **Invocation of Moloch** by Christiane Kliemannel - **Invocation of Satan** by Christiane Kliemannel - **Thaumiel: The Mask of Arrogance as Freedom** by Leonard Dewar - **The Calling of the Twin God** by Rev Bill Duvendack - **The Two-Headed Dragon of Thaumiel** by Leonard Dewar - **Invocation of the Lord of Thaumiel** by Rev Bill Duvendack - **Three Hidden Chakras Working** by Christiane Kliemannel

ISBN-10: 1530016320
ISBN-13: 978-1530016327

LILITH: DARK FEMININE ARCHETYPE

This anthology brings together essays, rituals, and unique artwork dedicated to the Queen of the Night and the Dark Goddess of the Qliphoth. Denied and rejected, worshipped and venerated, Lilith has been a part of the Western culture for ages. Viewed both as a beautiful seductress and a ruthless demon, she is the Serpent in the Garden of Eden, the first woman, and the primary initiatrix into the mysteries of the dark side of the Qabalistic Tree of Life. Her rites are the works of love and pain, sex and transgression, transcendence and immanence, for she exists at the roots of all desire of all humans past, present, and future. This archetype has never been fully grasped in its profundity and is constantly unfolding, challenging us to recognize our fears and passions and to transform them into tools of power. In this book you will find personal accounts of practitioners who ventured into the sacred and unholy garden of the Dark Queen of Sitra Ahra and returned transformed and empowered by her gnosis. Spells and invocations, dream magic and guided meditations, visions and stories of intimate encounters with Lilith - all this is contained in this unique anthology, written from the perspective of the Left Hand Path and the Draconian Tradition.

Asenath Mason: Introduction - Mike King: Sea of Ecstasy - Kai'Nathera: A Mother's Embrace - Asenath Mason & Rev Bill Duvendack: Fire and Lust - Martha Gray: Lilith and the Dual Nature of the Owl - Nemo.V: The Vase of Lilith - Katie Anderson: The Creative Fire: An Invocation to Lilith - Edgar Kerval: The Hidden Masks (A Lilith Exploration) - Rev Bill Duvendack: The Dark Feminine, a Man's Tale - Asenath Mason: The Unholy Grail - Mike King: Black Moon Lilith - Selene-Lilith: Selenic Face of Lilith - Greg Brown (aka Ahohlan): Journey into the Womb of Lilith - Alisa Jones: Lilith Queen of Tehiru Space - Asenath Mason: Lilith, Samael & Leviathan - Leonard Dewar: The Inconceivable Nature of Lilith - Lucien von Wolfe: Awakening the Vampire Within - Rev Bill Duvendack: The Mother of Abortions - Asenath Mason: The Mask of Medusa - Rev Bill Duvendack: Temple Astrological Correspondences

ISBN-10: 1979323267
ISBN-13: 978-1979323260

SET: THE FURY OF EGYPT

As a self-created god, Set is a powerful archetype of the Adversary and an attractive model for a practitioner seeking initiation into mysteries of self-deification. Feared by the faint-hearted and worshipped by those who sought power, he has become a symbol of storm and change, movement and transformation, force and energy. His fiery nature represents lust and fury, which is the driving force on the path, and his Black Flame is the inner spark of Godhood that successively becomes the fiery pillar of ascent on the path of self-initiation. His forked knife cuts attachments to the surrounding world, liberating the initiate from bonds of slavery and mindless ignorance, and his scepter represents authority and power, showing us how to devour our gods and be the masters of our destiny. These portrayals of Set and many more are the subject of this anthology. Essays and poetry, portraits and sigil art, rituals and meditations – all these contribute to the portrayal of Set as a god that is still alive and active in modern times, perhaps even more than ever before. We will look into his origins, ancient myths and legends, and modern interpretations of his role on the Left Hand Path – all this written from the perspective of the Draconian Tradition.

Asenath Mason: Lord of Storm and Change - **Bill Duvendack:** Fragments and Figments - **Edgar Kerval:** Hymns of Adoration to Setekh - **Mimi Hazim:** My Journey into the Desert with Set - **Fra Diavolo:** The Role of Set in Western Occultism - **Fra Diavolo:** The Ritual of Set-Transformation - **Soror Sortela:** Breaking Boundaries: A Sexual Encounter with Set - **Asenath Mason:** The Flaming Star of Set - **Asenath Mason:** The Many Faces of Set - **Bill Duvendack:** Set: An Astrological Portrait - **Cătălina Deaconu:** Baptized in the Ecstasy of Poison - **Mimi Hazim:** The Gift of Demise - **Keona Kai'Nathera:** Walking with Set - **Asenath Mason:** The Lord of Fire - **V. Ghallego-Iglesias:** Rising up in the Middle of the Sandstorm - **Bill Duvendack:** The Gods of the Underworld - **Asenath Mason:** Set and Nephthys: Chaos and Void - SPECIAL CONTRIBUTION: **Michael W. Ford, Akhtya Dahak Azal'ucel, Sasutekhwoser V°, Priest of Heka, Priest of Set** - EGYPTIAN LEFT-HAND PATH MAGICK: The Neter Set and the Black Alchemy of the Ba and Ka

ISBN-10: 1798163535
ISBN-13: 978-1798163535